The Ultimate Guide to Canadian Immigration Pathways

Gloria Morenike Faluyi-Ogieva

Published by KA Publishing Press Ltd, 2024.

While every precaution has been taken in the preparation of this book, the publisher assumes no responsibility for errors or omissions, or for damages resulting from the use of the information contained herein.

THE ULTIMATE GUIDE TO CANADIAN IMMIGRATION PATHWAYS

First edition. March 15, 2024.

ISBN: 979-8224797271

Written by Gloria Morenike Faluyi-Ogieva.

Table of Contents

I dedicate this book to God who has been my help all through my life and my sure hope till the end. Also to my lovely family who have always stood by me through thick and thin.

Introduction

WELCOME TO THIS BOOK on how to immigrate to Canada. In this book, you will learn about the different ways and steps to immigrate to Canada as a permanent resident or a temporary resident with the intention of becoming a permanent resident. You will also learn about the benefits and challenges of living in Canada, the rights and responsibilities of a Canadian citizen, and the resources and tips for settling in Canada.

Canada is a country of diversity and multiculturalism, where people from different backgrounds, cultures, religions, and languages live together in harmony. Canada is also a country of opportunity and prosperity, where people can enjoy a high quality of life, a strong economy, a stable democracy, and a safe environment. Canada is also a country of immigration and citizenship, where people can become permanent residents or citizens and contribute to Canadian society.

Canada is also one of the most popular destinations for immigrants in the world. According to the United Nations, Canada ranked ninth among the countries with the highest number of international migrants in 20201. Some of the reasons why people choose to immigrate to Canada are:

● Canada is a safe and peaceful country with a stable democracy and a respect for human rights.

● Canada is a diverse and multicultural country that welcomes people from all backgrounds and celebrates their contributions.

● Canada is a prosperous and innovative country that offers a high quality of life and a range of economic opportunities.

- Canada is a beautiful and natural country that boasts a variety of landscapes and climates.

- Canada is a bilingual and bilingual country that recognizes English and French as its official languages.

Immigrating to Canada is not an easy or simple process. It requires planning, preparation, patience, and perseverance. It also requires meeting various requirements and criteria, such as language skills, education level, work experience, financial situation, etc. However, immigrating to Canada is also a rewarding and fulfilling process. It offers many benefits and opportunities for you and your family, such as living in a diverse and multicultural society, accessing health care and social services, applying for Canadian citizenship, etc.

This book will help you with your immigration process by providing you with information and guidance on how to immigrate to Canada.

By the end of this book, you will have a better understanding of how to immigrate to Canada and what to expect from your immigration process. You will also have more confidence and motivation to pursue your immigration goals and start your new life in Canada.

This book is designed for anyone who is interested in immigrating to Canada or learning more about the Canadian immigration system. This book is not intended to provide legal advice or representation for your immigration application. You should always consult with an immigration consultant or lawyer if you need professional help with your immigration application.

This book is also designed for self-paced learning. You can take this book at your own pace and time. You can also skip or revisit any Chapter or section that you want. You can also use the online tools provided by IRCC on their website to access more information and resources related to your immigration application.

THE ULTIMATE GUIDE TO CANADIAN IMMIGRATION PATHWAYS

We hope that you enjoy this book and find it useful for your immigration process. We wish you all the best in your immigration journey and your new life in Canada. Thank you for taking this book. Let's begin!

Chapter 1: Understanding the Canadian Immigration System

Section 1: The Basics of Canadian Immigration

IF YOU ARE THINKING about immigrating to Canada, you might be wondering how the Canadian immigration system works and what are the different options available for you. In this section, we will cover the basics of Canadian immigration and help you understand the main concepts and terms that you will encounter throughout your immigration journey.

What is immigration and citizenship?

Let's start with some basic definitions. What is immigration and what is citizenship?

Immigration is the process of moving to a new country to live there permanently or temporarily. People who immigrate to a new country are called **immigrants**. Immigrants usually have different reasons for immigrating, such as :

• Seeking better opportunities for themselves and their families

• Pursuing education or career goals

• Reuniting with loved ones

• Escaping persecution, violence, or hardship

• Exploring new cultures and experiences

Citizenship is the legal status of being a member of a country. People who have citizenship of a country are called **citizens**. Citizens usually have certain rights and responsibilities in their country, such as voting, paying taxes, serving in the military, or travelling with a passport.

In Canada, immigration and citizenship are two separate things. You can immigrate to Canada without becoming a citizen, and you can become a citizen without immigrating to Canada. For example, you can immigrate to Canada as a permanent resident or a temporary resident, but you will not automatically become a citizen. You will have to apply for citizenship after meeting certain requirements. On the other hand, you can become a citizen without immigrating to Canada if you were born outside Canada to a Canadian parent or if you were adopted by a Canadian parent.

What are the types of immigration to Canada?

There are two main types of immigration to Canada: temporary and permanent.

Temporary immigration means that you come to Canada for a limited period of time, usually for a specific purpose, such as visiting, studying, working, or seeking asylum. Temporary immigrants need to have a valid document that allows them to enter and stay in Canada, such as a visa, an electronic travel authorization (eTA), or a permit. Temporary immigrants are also subject to certain conditions and restrictions, such as the duration and purpose of their stay, the type and amount of work they can do, and the need to leave Canada when their document expires or is revoked.

Permanent immigration means that you come to Canada with the intention of settling here permanently. Permanent immigrants are also known as permanent residents or landed immigrants. Permanent residents have the right to live, work, study, and access social services anywhere in Canada. They also have certain obligations, such as paying taxes, obeying the law, and respecting Canadian values. Permanent residents can apply for Canadian citizenship after meeting certain criteria, such as living in Canada for a minimum number of years, demonstrating language proficiency, passing a citizenship test, and taking an oath of allegiance.

Who is in charge of immigration in Canada?

In Canada, immigration is managed by two levels of government: the federal government and the provincial governments.

The **federal government** is the national government that represents all Canadians. The federal government is responsible for setting the overall immigration policies and laws, determining the number and type of immigrants that Canada accepts each year, processing immigration applications, issuing visas and permits, conducting security checks and medical exams, conducting interviews and landing procedures, providing pre-arrival and post-arrival services and programs, and granting citizenship.

The federal government's main department that deals with immigration is called **Immigration, Refugees and Citizenship Canada (IRCC)**. IRCC is led by a minister who is appointed by the prime minister. IRCC has offices across Canada and around the world where you can submit your application, pay your fees, take your language test, do your medical exam, attend your interview, or get your visa or permit.

The **provincial governments** are the regional governments that represent each province or territory in Canada. There are 10 provinces and 3 territories in Canada. The provincial governments are responsible for setting their own immigration policies and laws that suit their specific needs and priorities, selecting immigrants that can contribute to their economic and social development, nominating immigrants for permanent residence through their own immigration programs, providing settlement and integration services and programs within their jurisdictions, and issuing provincial health cards and driver's licenses.

Each province or territory has its own department or ministry that deals with immigration. For example, in Ontario, it is called the Ministry **of Labour, Training and Skills Development (MLTSD)**. In Alberta, it is called the Ministry **of Labour and Immigration (MLI)**. Each province or territory also has its own immigration program that works with IRCC. For example, in Ontario, it is called **Ontario Immigrant Nominee Program (OINP)**. In Alberta, it is called **Alberta Immigrant Nominee Program (AINP)**.

The federal government and the provincial governments work together to manage immigration in Canada through various agreements and partnerships. For example, one of the most important agreements is called **Canada-Quebec Accord**, which gives Quebec more autonomy and control over its own immigration program. Another example is called **Atlantic Immigration Pilot (AIP)**, which is a partnership between the federal government and four Atlantic provinces (New Brunswick, Nova Scotia, Prince Edward Island, and Newfoundland and Labrador) to attract more immigrants to their regions.

What are the types of residence status you can have in Canada?

When you immigrate to Canada, you will have a certain type of residence status that defines your rights and obligations in Canada. There are two main types of residence status you can have in Canada: permanent residence and temporary residence.

THE ULTIMATE GUIDE TO CANADIAN IMMIGRATION PATHWAYS

Permanent residence is the status of being allowed to live and work in Canada indefinitely. Permanent residents have most of the same rights and responsibilities as citizens, except they cannot vote, run for office, or hold certain jobs that require a high-level security clearance. Permanent residents also have to meet certain residency obligations to maintain their status, such as living in Canada for at least two years in a five-year period. Permanent residents can apply for citizenship after meeting certain requirements, such as living in Canada for at least three years in a five-year period, passing a language test and a citizenship test, and taking an oath of allegiance.

Temporary residence is the status of being allowed to live and work in Canada for a limited period of time. Temporary residents have fewer rights and responsibilities than permanent residents, and they have to follow the conditions and restrictions of their visas or permits. Temporary residents cannot apply for citizenship, but they can apply for permanent residence through certain immigration programs, such as Express Entry or Provincial Nominee Program. Temporary residents include visitors, students, workers, and refugees.

Visitors are people who come to Canada for a short period of time for tourism, business, or family reasons. Visitors need a valid passport and a visitor visa or an electronic travel authorization (ETA) to enter Canada, unless they are from a visa-exempt country. Visitors can stay in Canada for up to six months, unless they are given a different duration by the border officer. Visitors cannot work or study in Canada without a permit.

Students are people who come to Canada to study at a designated learning institution (DLI), such as a school, college, or university. Students need a valid passport and a study permit to enter and stay in Canada. Students can work part-time on or off campus while studying, and full-time during scheduled breaks, without a work permit.

Students can also apply for a post-graduation work permit (PGWP) after completing their studies, which allows them to work in Canada for up to three years.

Workers are people who come to Canada to work for a Canadian employer or as a self-employed person. Workers need a valid passport and a work permit to enter and stay in Canada. Workers can only work for the employer, or the occupation specified on their work permit, unless they have an open work permit that allows them to work for any employer or occupation. Workers can also bring their spouse or partner and dependent children with them to Canada, and they may be eligible for a spouse or partner work permit or a study permit for their children.

Refugees are people who come to Canada to seek protection from persecution, violence, or human rights violations in their home country. Refugees can make their claim either outside Canada through the United Nations Refugee Agency (UNHCR) or inside Canada at the port of entry or at an IRCC office. Refugees need a valid passport and a refugee visa or an asylum seeker document to enter and stay in Canada. Refugees can work and study in Canada with a work permit or a study permit while waiting for their claim decision, once their claim is approved, they become Protected Persons. Protected Persons can also apply for permanent residence after their claim has been approved by the Immigration and Refugee Board of Canada (IRB).

What are the main categories and subcategories of immigration programs you can apply for?

When you want to immigrate to Canada, you will have to choose an immigration program that suits your situation and goals. There are many immigration programs you can apply for, but they can be grouped into three main categories: economic immigration, family immigration, and humanitarian immigration.

THE ULTIMATE GUIDE TO CANADIAN IMMIGRATION PATHWAYS

Economic immigration is the category of immigration programs that are designed to attract immigrants who can contribute to Canada's economy through their skills, education, work experience, language ability, or business acumen. Economic immigration programs include:

- **Federal economic immigration programs**: These are the programs that are managed by IRCC under the Express Entry system. They include:

  o **Federal Skilled Worker Program (FSWP)**: This program is for skilled workers who have at least one year of full-time paid work experience in an occupation that is in demand in Canada.

  o **Federal Skilled Trades Program (FSTP)**: This program is for skilled tradespeople who have at least two years of full-time paid work experience in an eligible trade occupation that is in demand in Canada.

  o **Canadian Experience Class (CEC)**: This program is for skilled workers who have at least one year of full-time paid work experience in Canada in an occupation that is in demand in Canada.

- **Provincial economic immigration programs**: These are the programs that are managed by provincial governments under the Provincial Nominee Program (PNP). They include:

  o **Express Entry-linked streams**: These are the streams that are aligned with the Express Entry system and allow provincial governments to nominate candidates from the Express Entry pool who meet their specific criteria.

o **Occupation-specific streams**: These are the streams that target specific occupations that are in demand in each province or territory.

o **Business streams**: These are the streams that target entrepreneurs, investors, or self-employed persons who want to start or invest in a business in each province or territory.

• **Other economic immigration programs**: These are the programs that are not managed by IRCC or provincial governments, but by other federal departments or agencies. They include:

o **Start-up Visa program**: This program is for entrepreneurs who have an innovative business idea that is supported by a designated organization, such as an angel investor, a venture capital fund, or a business incubator.

o **Self-Employed Persons program**: This program is for self-employed persons who have relevant experience and can make a significant contribution to Canada's cultural or athletic life, such as artists, athletes, or coaches.

o **Agri-Food Pilot program**: This program is for workers who have experience in specific agri-food occupations and industries, such as meat processing, mushroom production, or greenhouse cultivation.

Family immigration is the category of immigration programs that are designed to reunite family members who are separated by immigration. Family immigration programs include:

• **Family Class Sponsorship program**: This program is for Canadian citizens or permanent residents who want to sponsor their eligible family members to come to Canada as permanent residents. Eligible family members include spouses, partners, children, parents, grandparents, and other relatives.

- **Spouse or Partner Work Permit program**: This program is for spouses or partners of temporary workers or students who want to come to Canada as temporary workers. Spouses or partners can apply for an open work permit that allows them to work for any employer or occupation in Canada.

- **Dependent Children Study Permit program**: This program is for dependent children of temporary workers or students who want to come to Canada as temporary students. Dependent children can apply for a study permit that allows them to study at any designated learning institution in Canada.

Humanitarian immigration is the category of immigration programs that are designed to protect people who are in need of humanitarian and compassionate consideration. Humanitarian immigration programs include:

- **Refugee and Asylum program**: This program is for people who are fleeing persecution, violence, or human rights violations in their home country and who need protection in Canada. Refugees and asylum seekers can make their claim either outside Canada through the United Nations Refugee Agency (UNHCR) or inside Canada at the port of entry or at an IRCC office.

- **Humanitarian and Compassionate Grounds program**: This program is for people who are already in Canada and who face unusual, undeserved, or disproportionate hardship if they have to leave Canada. Humanitarian and compassionate grounds applicants can apply for permanent residence based on their exceptional circumstances that warrant special consideration from IRCC.

What are some key terms and concepts related to Canadian immigration?

There are many terms and concepts that you will encounter when you learn about Canadian immigration. Here are some of the most common ones that you should know:

• Status: Your status refers to your legal position or category in Canada. For example, you can have a status as a citizen, a permanent resident, a temporary resident (visitor, student, worker), or an asylum seeker.

• Category: Your category refers to your specific type or class of immigration within your status. For example, if you are a permanent resident, you can belong to one of three categories: economic immigration, family reunification, or humanitarian considerations.

• Program: Your program refers to your specific pathway or option of immigration within your category. For example, if you are an economic immigrant, you can apply through one of several programs, such as Express Entry, Provincial Nominee Program (PNP), or Start-up Visa Program.

• Stream: Your stream refers to your specific sub-category or variation of immigration within your program. For example, if you apply through Express Entry, you can choose one of three streams: Federal Skilled Worker Program (FSWP), Federal Skilled Trades Program (FSTP), or Canadian Experience Class (CEC).

In the next section, I will explain one of the most popular and competitive economic immigration programs: the Express Entry system. Let's go!

Section 2: The Express Entry System

What is the Express Entry system and how does it work?

Express Entry is a system used by the Canadian government to manage and process applications for permanent residence from skilled workers who want to contribute to Canada's economy. It is an online system that IRCC uses to manage immigration applications from skilled workers who want to immigrate to Canada permanently. It was launched in January 2015 to replace the previous first-come, first-served system that was slow, inefficient, and prone to backlogs.

The main goals of Express Entry are to:

• Attract and select the best and brightest immigrants who can meet Canada's labour market needs and integrate successfully.

• Reduce the processing time for permanent residence applications to six months or less.

• Increase the flexibility and responsiveness of the immigration system to changing economic conditions and priorities.

• Align the immigration system with the needs and preferences of employers, provinces, and territories.

The system manages three federal economic immigration programs: Federal Skilled Worker Program (FSWP), Federal Skilled Trades Program (FSTP), and Canadian Experience Class (CEC). These programs are designed to attract immigrants who have skills, education, work experience, and language ability that are in demand in Canada.

The Express Entry system works in four steps:

• Step 1: Find out if you are eligible for one or more of the Express Entry programs. You will have to answer some questions online about your personal information, such as your age, education, work experience, language skills, etc. Based on your answers, IRCC will tell you which programs you qualify for and what are the minimum requirements you need to meet.

• Step 2: Create an Express Entry profile and enter the pool of candidates. If you are eligible for one or more of the Express Entry programs, you can create an online profile where you provide more details about yourself. You will also need to upload some documents, such as language test results, education assessments, etc. Once you submit your profile, IRCC will give you a CRS score based on various factors, such as your skills, education, work experience, language ability, etc. Your CRS score will determine your rank in the pool of candidates. The higher your score, the higher your rank.

• Step 3: Improve your CRS score and increase your chances of receiving an ITA. IRCC regularly invites candidates from the pool to apply for permanent residence based on their CRS score and other criteria. The number and frequency of invitations depend on various factors, such as the immigration targets, the demand for certain occupations, etc. IRCC publishes the minimum CRS score and the number of invitations for each round of invitations on its website. If you want to receive an ITA, you need to have a CRS score above or equal to the minimum score for your round of invitations. You can improve your CRS score by improving your language skills, gaining more work experience, obtaining a job offer or a provincial nomination, etc.

• Step 4: Apply for permanent residence after receiving an ITA. If you receive an ITA from IRCC, you can apply for permanent residence online within 60 days. You will have to fill out some application forms and pay some application fees. You will also have to submit some supporting documents, such as police certificates, medical exams, proof of funds, etc. IRCC will process your application and make a decision within six months or less. If your application is approved, IRCC will issue you a confirmation of permanent residence (COPR) and a permanent resident visa (if applicable). You can then travel to Canada and complete your landing process at the port of entry or at a local IRCC office.

These are the four steps of the Express Entry system and how it works. Next, I will explain each step in more detail and provide you with some tips and resources to help you succeed in each step.

What are the eligibility criteria and requirements for the three federal economic immigration programs under Express Entry?

As I mentioned before, the Express Entry system manages three federal economic immigration programs: FSWP, FSTP, and CEC. Each program has its own eligibility criteria and requirements that you need to meet in order to qualify. In this subsection, I will describe the eligibility criteria and requirements for each program.

Federal Skilled Worker Program (FSWP)

The FSWP is for skilled workers who have at least one year of full-time paid work experience in an occupation that is in demand in Canada. To be eligible for this program, you need to meet the following criteria:

- You need to have at least one year of continuous full-time or equivalent part-time paid work experience in a skilled occupation (NOC 0, A or B) in the last 10 years. The work experience must be relevant to the occupation you want to perform in Canada. You also need to provide proof of your work experience, such as reference letters, pay stubs, tax returns, etc.

• You need to have a minimum level of language proficiency in English or French. You need to take a language test from an approved agency and score at least Canadian Language Benchmark (CLB) 7 in all four abilities (listening, speaking, reading and writing). You also need to provide your test results with your profile. Your test results must be less than two years old when you apply.

• You need to have a minimum level of education. You need to have a Canadian secondary or post-secondary certificate, diploma or degree, or an equivalent foreign credential. You also need to have an Educational Credential Assessment (ECA) report from an approved agency that shows that your foreign credential is valid and equal to a Canadian one. You also need to provide your ECA report with your profile. Your ECA report must be less than five years old when you apply.

• You need to have enough money to support yourself and your family in Canada. You need to show that you have enough funds to cover your living expenses for the first six months after you arrive in Canada. The amount of money you need depends on the size of your family and is updated every year by IRCC. You also need to provide proof of your funds, such as bank statements, letters from financial institutions, etc.

• You need to meet the admissibility requirements. You need to pass the security checks and medical exams that IRCC requires for all immigrants. You also need to have a clean criminal record and not be involved in any human or international rights violations.

These are the eligibility criteria and requirements for the FSWP. If you meet these criteria and requirements, you can apply for this program through the Express Entry system. However, meeting these criteria and requirements does not guarantee that you will receive an ITA or be approved for permanent residence. You will still have to compete with other candidates in the pool based on your CRS score and other factors.

Federal Skilled Trades Program (FSTP)

The FSTP is for skilled tradespeople who have at least two years of full-time paid work experience in an eligible trade occupation that is in demand in Canada. To be eligible for this program, you need to meet the following criteria:

• You need to have at least two years of full-time or equivalent part-time paid work experience in a skilled trade occupation (NOC B) in the last five years. The work experience must be relevant to the trade occupation you want to perform in Canada. You also need to provide proof of your work experience, such as reference letters, pay stubs, tax returns, etc.

• You need to have a valid job offer of full-time employment for a total period of at least one year from up to two employers in Canada or a certificate of qualification in your trade occupation from a Canadian provincial or territorial authority. The job offer or the certificate of qualification must be related to the trade occupation you want to perform in Canada. You also need to provide proof of your job offer or certificate of qualification with your profile.

• You need to have a minimum level of language proficiency in English or French. You need to take a language test from an approved agency and score at least CLB 5 for speaking and listening and CLB 4 for reading and writing. You also need to provide your test results with your profile. Your test results must be less than two years old when you apply.

• You need to meet the admissibility requirements. You need to pass the security checks and medical exams that IRCC requires for all immigrants. You also need to have a clean criminal record and not be involved in any human or international rights violations.

These are the eligibility criteria and requirements for the FSTP. If you meet these criteria and requirements, you can apply for this program through the Express Entry system. However, meeting these criteria and requirements does not guarantee that you will receive an ITA or be approved for permanent residence. You will still have to compete with other candidates in the pool based on your CRS score and other factors.

Canadian Experience Class (CEC)

The CEC is for skilled workers who have at least one year of full-time paid work experience in Canada in an occupation that is in demand in Canada. To be eligible for this program, you need to meet the following criteria:

• You need to have at least one year of continuous full-time or equivalent part-time paid work experience in Canada in a skilled occupation (NOC 0, A or B) in the last three years. The work experience must be gained while you had a valid temporary status as a worker or student in Canada. You also need to provide proof of your work experience, such as reference letters, pay stubs, tax returns, etc.

• You need to have a minimum level of language proficiency in English or French. You need to take.

• You need to take a language test from an approved agency and score at least CLB 7 for NOC 0 or A occupations or CLB 5 for NOC B occupations in all four abilities. You also need to provide your test results with your profile. Your test results must be less than two years old when you apply.

• You need to meet the admissibility requirements. You need to pass the security checks and medical exams that IRCC requires for all immigrants. You also need to have a clean criminal record and not be involved in any human or international rights violations.

These are the eligibility criteria and requirements for the CEC. If you meet these criteria and requirements, you can apply for this program through the Express Entry system. However, meeting these criteria and requirements does not guarantee that you will receive an ITA or be approved for permanent residence. You will still have to compete with other candidates in the pool based on your CRS score and other factors.

Up next, I will explain how to create an Express Entry profile and enter the pool of candidates. Let's go!

How to create an Express Entry profile and enter the pool of candidates?

If you are eligible for one or more of the Express Entry programs, you can create an Express Entry profile and enter the pool of candidates. This is the first step of applying for Canadian immigration through the Express Entry system.

What is an Express Entry profile and what is the pool of candidates?

An Express Entry profile is an online form where you provide information about yourself, such as your personal details, education, work experience, language skills, etc. You can create an Express Entry profile on IRCC's website using your personal reference code (if you have one) or by creating a new account. You will need a valid passport, a language test result, an education assessment report (if applicable), and a job offer or a provincial nomination (if applicable) to create your profile.

The pool of candidates is a database where IRCC stores all the Express Entry profiles that are active and valid. IRCC uses the pool of candidates to select and invite candidates to apply for permanent residence based on their CRS score and other criteria. Your CRS score is a number between 0 and 1200 that reflects your human capital factors, such as your skills, education, work experience, language ability, etc. The higher your CRS score, the higher your rank in the pool of candidates. The lower your CRS score, the lower your rank in the pool of candidates.

How to create an Express Entry profile and enter the pool of candidates?

To create an Express Entry profile and enter the pool of candidates, you need to follow these steps:

• Step 1: Gather your documents and information. You need to have the following documents and information ready before you start creating your profile:

  o A valid passport or travel document

  o A language test result from an approved agency (IELTS, CELPIP, or TEF) that is less than two years old.

  o An education credential assessment (ECA) report from an approved agency (WES, ICAS, IQAS, etc.) that shows that your foreign credential is valid and equal to a Canadian one (if applicable) o A job offer letter from a Canadian employer or a certificate of qualification from a Canadian provincial or territorial authority (if applicable)

o A nomination certificate or letter from a Canadian province or territory (if applicable)

o A personal reference code from IRCC's online tool "Come to Canada" (if you have one)

• Step 2: Create an online account on IRCC's website. You need to create an online account on IRCC's website where you can access and manage your Express Entry profile. You can use your personal reference code (if you have one) or create a new account using your email address and password. You will also need to answer some security questions and agree to some terms and conditions.

• Step 3: Fill out your Express Entry profile. You need to fill out your Express Entry profile online using your online account. You will have to answer some questions about yourself, such as your personal details, education, work experience, language skills, etc. You will also have to upload some documents, such as your language test results, education assessments, job offer letters, etc. You will have to provide accurate and complete information that matches your documents. If you provide false or misleading information, IRCC may refuse your application or ban you from applying for five years.

• Step 4: Submit your Express Entry profile. You need to submit your Express Entry profile online using your online account. Once you submit your profile, IRCC will review it and check if you are eligible for one or more of the Express Entry programs. If you are eligible, IRCC will give you a CRS score based on the information you provided in your profile. Your CRS score will determine your rank in the pool of candidates. If you are not eligible, IRCC will tell you why and what you can do to improve your eligibility.

• Step 5: Enter the pool of candidates. If you are eligible and have submitted your Express Entry profile, you will automatically enter the pool of candidates. You will receive a confirmation message from IRCC with your CRS score and other details. You will also receive regular updates from IRCC about the rounds of invitations and the minimum CRS score required for each round.

These are the steps to create an Express Entry profile and enter the pool of candidates. Next, I will explain how to improve your Comprehensive Ranking System (CRS) score and increase your chances of receiving an Invitation to Apply (ITA) from IRCC.

What is the Comprehensive Ranking System (CRS) and how does it work?

The Comprehensive Ranking System (CRS) is a points-based system that IRCC uses to rank and select candidates from the pool of candidates based on their human capital factors, such as their skills, education, work experience, language ability, etc. The CRS also considers some additional factors, such as having a job offer or a provincial nomination, having a sibling in Canada, or having French language skills. The CRS assigns a score between 0 and 1200 to each candidate based on these factors. The higher your CRS score, the higher your rank in the pool of candidates. The lower your CRS score, the lower your rank in the pool of candidates.

The CRS score is divided into two parts: core points and additional points. The core points account for up to 600 points and are based on four factors: skills and experience, spouse or partner factors, skills transferability, and additional points for Canadian degrees, diplomas or certificates. The additional points account for up to 600 points and are based on five factors: having a provincial nomination, having a valid job offer, having a sibling in Canada, having French language skills, and having post-secondary education in Canada.

The CRS score is dynamic and can change over time depending on your personal circumstances and the pool of candidates. For example, your CRS score can increase if you improve your language skills, gain more work experience, obtain a job offer or a provincial nomination, etc. Your CRS score can also decrease if you lose your job offer or provincial nomination, age out of a certain age group, etc. Your CRS score can also be affected by the changes in the pool of candidates, such as the number and quality of candidates, the frequency and size of invitations, etc.

The CRS score is the main factor that determines whether you will receive an ITA from IRCC or not. IRCC regularly invites candidates from the pool to apply for permanent residence based on their CRS score and other criteria. The number and frequency of invitations depend on various factors, such as the immigration targets, the demand for certain occupations, etc. IRCC publishes the minimum CRS score and the number of invitations for each round of invitations on its website. If you want to receive an ITA from IRCC, you need to have a CRS score above or equal to the minimum score for your round of invitations.

How to improve your CRS score and increase your chances of receiving an ITA from IRCC?

If you want to improve your CRS score and increase your chances of receiving an ITA from IRCC, you need to focus on the factors that can boost your CRS score the most. These factors include:

• Having a provincial nomination: This is the most effective way to increase your CRS score by 600 points. If you receive a provincial nomination from a province or territory through one of their PNP streams, you will automatically get 600 additional points added to your CRS score. This means that you will almost certainly receive an ITA from IRCC in the next round of invitations. However, getting a provincial nomination is not easy and requires meeting specific criteria and requirements that vary depending on the province or territory. You also need to submit an expression of interest (EOI) or an application for a provincial nomination through one of their PNP streams online or by mail.

• Having a valid job offer: This is another effective way to increase your CRS score by up to 200 points. If you have a valid job offer from a Canadian employer in an eligible occupation that is consistent with your skills and training, you will get 50 or 200 additional points added to your CRS score depending on the skill level or type of the occupation. However, getting a valid job offer is not easy and requires meeting specific criteria and requirements that vary depending on the type of job offer. You also need to provide proof of your job offer letter with your profile.

• Having a sibling in Canada: This is a simple way to increase your CRS score by 15 points. If you have a sibling who is a Canadian citizen or permanent resident living in Canada who is at least 18 years old, you will get 15 additional points added to your CRS score. However, having a sibling in Canada is not something that you can control or change easily. You also need to provide proof of your relationship with your sibling with your profile.

• Having French language skills: This is another simple way to increase your CRS score by up to 30 points. If you have French language skills in addition to English language skills, you will get up to 30 additional points added to your CRS score depending on your level of proficiency in both languages. However, having French language skills is not something that you can acquire or improve quickly. You also need to take a language test from an approved agency (TEF or TCF) and provide your test results with your profile.

• Having post-secondary education in Canada: This is a less common way to increase your CRS score by up to 30 points. If you have a Canadian degree, diploma or certificate from a Canadian educational institution, you will get up to 30 additional points added to your CRS score depending on the level and duration of your education. However, having post-secondary education in Canada.

These are some of the factors that can improve your CRS score and increase your chances of receiving an ITA from IRCC. However, these factors are not the only ones that affect your CRS score. There are other factors that can also influence your CRS score, such as:

• Your age: Your age can affect your CRS score positively or negatively depending on which age group you belong to. The maximum points you can get for your age are 110 points if you are between 20 and 29 years old. The minimum points you can get for your age are 0 points if you are over 45 years old.

• Your spouse or partner's factors: If you have a spouse or partner who will accompany you to Canada, their factors can also affect your CRS score positively or negatively depending on their skills, education, work experience, language ability, etc. The maximum points you can get for your spouse or partner's factors are 40 points if they have high levels of human capital factors. The minimum points you can get for your spouse or partner's factors are 0 points if they have low levels of human capital factors.

• Your skills transferability: Your skills transferability refers to how well you can combine and use two or more human capital factors together, such as education and language skills, work experience and language skills, etc. The maximum points you can get for your skills transferability are 100 points if you have high levels of combination factors. The minimum points you can get for your skills transferability are 0 points if you have low levels of combination factors.

Trust you are following closely. Next, I will explain how to apply for permanent residence after receiving an ITA from IRCC.

How to apply for permanent residence after receiving an ITA from IRCC?

If you receive an ITA from IRCC, you can apply for permanent residence online within 60 days. This is the final step of applying for Canadian immigration through the Express Entry system. In this subsection, I will explain how to apply for permanent residence after receiving an ITA from IRCC. I will also provide you with some tips and resources to help you prepare and submit your application successfully.

What is an ITA and how to accept it?

An ITA is a letter or message that IRCC sends to candidates from the pool who have a CRS score above or equal to the minimum score for their round of invitations. An ITA means that IRCC has invited you to apply for permanent residence through one of the Express Entry programs. An ITA also indicates which Express Entry program you are invited to apply for, such as FSWP, FSTP, or CEC.

To accept your ITA, you need to follow these steps:

• Step 1: Log in to your online account on IRCC's website. You need to log in to your online account where you can access and manage your Express Entry profile and application. You will see a notification that you have received an ITA from IRCC.

• Step 2: Confirm your interest in applying for permanent residence. You need to confirm that you are interested in applying for permanent residence through the Express Entry program that you are invited to apply for. You will have to answer some questions about your personal information, such as your name, date of birth, passport number, etc. You will also have to agree to some terms and conditions.

• Step 3: Receive your application package and instructions. Once you confirm your interest in applying for permanent residence, IRCC will send you an application package and instructions on how to complete and submit your application online. The application package will include some application forms that you need to fill out and some supporting documents that you need to upload.

These are the steps to accept your ITA from IRCC. You will have 60 days from the date of your ITA to complete and submit your application online. If you do not accept your ITA or submit your application within 60 days, your ITA will expire and you will lose your chance to apply for permanent residence. You will also have to re-enter the pool of candidates and wait for another ITA from IRCC.

How to complete and submit your application for permanent residence online?

To complete and submit your application for permanent residence online, you need to follow these steps:

- Step 1: Fill out your application forms online. You need to fill out your application forms online using your online account. The application forms will ask you some questions about yourself and your family members, such as your personal details, education, work experience, language skills, etc. You will also have to declare any changes or updates in your information since you submitted your Express Entry profile. You will have to provide accurate and complete information that matches your supporting documents. If you provide false or misleading information, IRCC may refuse your application or ban you from applying for five years.

- Step 2: Pay your application fees online. You need to pay your application fees online using your online account. The application fees include the processing fee, the right of permanent residence fee (RPRF), and the biometric fee (if applicable). The processing fee is $825 CAD per person for the principal applicant and each family member who is 22 years old or older, and $225 CAD per person for each family member who is under 22 years old. The RPRF is $500 CAD per person for the principal applicant and each family member who is 22 years old or older, and $0 CAD per person for each family member who is under 22 years old. The biometric fee is $85 CAD per person or $170 CAD per family (up to two people). You can pay your fees by credit card, debit card, or prepaid card.

- Step 3: Upload your supporting documents online. You need to upload your supporting documents online using your online account. The supporting documents include proof of identity, proof of education, proof of work experience, proof of language skills, proof of funds, proof of medical exams, proof of police certificates, proof of job offer or provincial nomination (if applicable), etc. You will also have to provide translations and certifications for any documents that are not in English or French. You will have to follow the specific format and size requirements that IRCC provides for each document.

• Step 4: Submit your application online. You need to submit your application online using your online account. Once you submit your application, IRCC will review it and check if it is complete and accurate. If your application is incomplete or inaccurate, IRCC may reject it or ask you to provide more information or documents. If your application is complete and accurate, IRCC will process it and make a decision within six months or less. If your application is approved, IRCC will issue you a confirmation of permanent residence (COPR) and a permanent resident visa (if applicable). You can then travel to Canada and complete your landing process at the port of entry or at a local IRCC office.

These are the steps to complete and submit your application for permanent residence online after receiving an ITA from IRCC. In the next section, I will explain the Provincial Nominee Program (PNP). Let's go!

Section 3: The Provincial Nominee Program (PNP)

Another way to immigrate to Canada as a skilled worker is through the provincial nominee programs (PNPs).

What is the PNP and how does it work?

The PNP is a immigration program operated by the Canadian provinces and territories in partnership with the federal government. This program allows the provinces and territories to nominate or select immigrants who have the skills, education, and work experience that match their specific economic and demographic needs. The PNP also gives immigrants more options and flexibility to choose where they want to live and work in Canada.

PNPs exist because Canada is a large and diverse country with different regions that have different needs and priorities. By giving the provinces and territories more control and flexibility over their immigration policies and programs, PNPs help to:

● Distribute the benefits and impacts of immigration across the country.

● Address the labour market shortages and gaps in different sectors and regions.

● Attract and retain immigrants who have a strong connection and commitment to their chosen province or territory.

● Support the economic development and social integration of immigrants and their communities.

The PNP works as follows:

THE ULTIMATE GUIDE TO CANADIAN IMMIGRATION PATHWAYS

- Step 1: Choose a province or territory. You need to research the different provinces and territories and their PNP streams to find out which one suits your needs and goals. You can use various sources of information, such as the official websites of the provinces and territories, online forums, blogs, or videos of other immigrants who have gone through the PNP process, or professional advice from an immigration consultant.

- Step 2: Apply for a provincial nomination through a PNP stream. Each province or territory has its own PNP that consists of various streams that target different types of immigrants, such as skilled workers, semi-skilled workers, international graduates, entrepreneurs, investors, etc. Each stream has its own eligibility criteria and requirements that you need to meet to qualify. You can apply for a provincial nomination through a PNP stream online or by mail, depending on the province or territory. You will have to fill out some application forms and pay some application fees. You will also have to submit some supporting documents, such as language test results, education assessments, job offer letters, etc.

- Step 3: Receive a nomination certificate. If your application is approved, you will receive a nomination certificate from the province or territory that confirms your nomination. A nomination certificate does not guarantee your permanent residence, but it gives you an advantage in the immigration process. Depending on the type of PNP stream, your nomination certificate may be valid for six months or one year.

- Step 4: Apply for permanent residence. After receiving a nomination certificate, you need to apply for permanent residence to the federal government. You need to submit an application with all the required documents and fees. You also need to pass a medical exam and a police check. The processing time for your permanent residence application may vary depending on the type of PNP stream, your personal situation, and other factors.

What are the types of PNP streams?

There are two types of PNP streams: base PNPs and enhanced PNPs.

Base PNPs are PNP streams that are not aligned with Express Entry. They operate independently from the federal immigration system. To apply for a base PNP stream, you need to:

• Apply directly to the province or territory that offers the stream.

• Meet the eligibility criteria and requirements of the stream.

• Receive a nomination certificate from the province or territory.

• Apply for permanent residence to IRCC using a paper-based application.

Base PNPs have their own application processes, selection criteria, quotas, and processing times. They may be more suitable for immigrants who do not qualify for Express Entry or who have lower CRS scores.

Enhanced PNPs are PNP streams that are aligned with Express Entry. They operate in conjunction with the federal immigration system. To apply for an enhanced PNP stream, you need to:

• Create an online Express Entry profile and indicate your interest in a province or territory.

• Meet the eligibility criteria and requirements of both Express Entry and the stream.

- Receive a notification of interest (NOI) from the province or territory.

- Apply for a nomination from the province or territory.

- Receive an invitation to apply (ITA) from IRCC

- Apply for permanent residence to IRCC using an online application.

Enhanced PNPs use Express Entry as a platform to manage applications, rank candidates, issue invitations, and process applications. They may be more suitable for immigrants who qualify for Express Entry and who have higher CRS scores.

Just to recap, PNPs are immigration programs that allow you to immigrate to Canada based on your connection and contribution to a specific province or territory. You can apply for a provincial nomination through a base PNP or an enhanced PNP depending on your situation and preferences. In both cases, you need to meet the eligibility criteria and requirements of both the province or territory and the federal government.

What are the different PNP streams and their eligibility criteria?

Express Entry-linked streams (Enhanced PNP)

These are the streams that are aligned with the Express Entry system and allow provincial governments to nominate candidates from the Express Entry pool who meet their specific criteria. These streams are also known as enhanced streams or aligned streams. These streams have two advantages:

- they can increase your CRS score by 600 points if you receive a provincial nomination, which virtually guarantees that you will receive an ITA from IRCC.

• and they can fast-track your permanent residence application process, as IRCC prioritizes Express Entry applications.

To be eligible for these streams, you need to meet the following criteria:

• You need to be eligible for one or more of the Express Entry programs (FSWP, FSTP, or CEC) and have an active Express Entry profile with a valid CRS score.

• You need to meet the minimum criteria and requirements of the specific Express Entry-linked stream that you are applying for. These criteria and requirements may vary depending on the province or territory, but they usually include factors such as your occupation, education, work experience, language skills, job offer, connection to the province or territory, etc.

• You need to submit an expression of interest (EOI) or an application for a provincial nomination through the specific Express Entry-linked stream that you are applying for. You may also need to pay some application fees or submit some supporting documents.

Some examples of Express Entry-linked streams are:

• **Ontario Human Capital Priorities Stream**: This stream is for skilled workers who have an active Express Entry profile with a CRS score of at least 400 points and who have work experience in one of the eligible occupations that are in demand in Ontario.

• **Alberta Express Entry Stream**: This stream is for skilled workers who have an active Express Entry profile with a CRS score of at least 300 points and who have work experience in an occupation that supports Alberta's economic development and diversification.

• **Nova Scotia Labour Market Priorities Stream**: This stream is for skilled workers who have an active Express Entry profile and who have work experience in one of the occupations that are in demand in Nova Scotia. The occupations are selected by the province based on the current labour market needs.

Occupation-specific streams (Base PnP)

These are the streams that target specific occupations that are in demand in each province or territory. These streams are also known as base streams or non-aligned streams. These streams do not require you to have an Express Entry profile, but they may have lower language or education requirements than the Express Entry programs. However, these streams may also have longer processing times and lower quotas than the Express Entry-linked streams.

To be eligible for these streams, you need to meet the following criteria:

• You need to have work experience in one of the eligible occupations that are in demand in the province or territory that you are applying for. The work experience must be relevant to the occupation that you want to perform in Canada. You also need to provide proof of your work experience, such as reference letters, pay stubs, tax returns, etc.

• You need to meet the minimum criteria and requirements of the specific occupation-specific stream that you are applying for. These criteria and requirements may vary depending on the province or territory, but they usually include factors such as your occupation, education, work experience, language skills, job offer, connection to the province or territory, etc.

• You need to submit an application for a provincial nomination through the specific occupation-specific stream that you are applying for. You may also need to pay some application fees or submit some supporting documents.

Some examples of occupation-specific streams are:

• **British Columbia Healthcare Professional Stream**: This stream is for healthcare professionals who have work experience in one of the eligible healthcare occupations that are in demand in British Columbia, such as physicians, nurses, allied health professionals, etc.

• **Manitoba Skilled Worker in Manitoba Stream**: This stream is for skilled workers who have work experience in Manitoba and who have a job offer from a Manitoba employer in an eligible occupation that is consistent with their skills and training.

• **Saskatchewan International Skilled Worker - Occupation In-Demand Stream**: This stream is for skilled workers who have work experience in one of the eligible occupations that are in demand in Saskatchewan, such as engineering, agriculture, health care, etc.

Business streams

These are the streams that target entrepreneurs, investors, or self-employed persons who want to start or invest in a business in each province or territory. These streams are also known as entrepreneur streams or investor streams. These streams require you to have a minimum net worth and investment amount, as well as a business plan and a performance agreement with the province or territory. These streams also require you to visit Canada and operate your business for a certain period of time before you can apply for permanent residence.

To be eligible for these streams, you need to meet the following criteria:

• You need to have a minimum net worth and investment amount that meets the requirements of the specific business stream that you are applying for. The net worth and investment amount may vary depending on the province or territory, but they usually range from $300,000 CAD to $2 million CAD.

• You need to have a business plan and a performance agreement with the province or territory that you are applying for. The business plan and performance agreement must outline your proposed business idea, your investment amount and source of funds, your expected economic benefits and outcomes, your management skills and experience, your market research and analysis, etc.

• You need to visit Canada and operate your business for a certain period of time before you can apply for permanent residence. The visit and operation period may vary depending on the province or territory, but they usually range from 6 months to 2 years.

Some examples of business streams are:

• **Ontario Entrepreneur Stream**: This stream is for entrepreneurs who want to start or buy a new or existing business in Ontario. The minimum net worth requirement is $800,000 CAD if your proposed business is located within the Greater Toronto Area (GTA) or $400,000 CAD if your proposed business is located outside the GTA. The minimum investment requirement is $600,000 CAD if your proposed business is located within the GTA or $200,000 CAD if your proposed business is located outside the GTA.

• **Alberta Self-Employed Farmer Stream**: This stream is for self-employed farmers who want to buy and manage a farm in Alberta. The minimum net worth requirement is $500,000 CAD. The minimum investment requirement is $500,000 CAD.

• **Nova Scotia Entrepreneur Stream**: This stream is for entrepreneurs who want to start or buy a new or existing business in Nova Scotia. The minimum net worth requirement is $600,000 CAD. The minimum investment requirement is $150,000 CAD.

These are some of the eligibility criteria and requirements for the different PNP streams across Canada. If you meet these criteria and requirements, you can apply for a provincial nomination through one of these PNP streams online or by mail.

However, meeting these criteria and requirements does not guarantee that you will receive a provincial nomination or be approved for permanent residence. You will still have to compete with other applicants in the PNP stream that you are applying for and meet the federal admissibility requirements. Therefore, it is important to prepare and submit your application carefully and accurately. In the next subsection, I will explain how to apply for a provincial nomination through a PNP stream online or by mail. Stay tuned!

How to apply for a provincial nomination through a PNP stream

If you are eligible for one of the PNP streams that I described in the previous subsection, you can apply for a provincial nomination through that stream online or by mail.

How to apply for a provincial nomination through a PNP stream online?

To apply for a provincial nomination through a PNP stream online, you need to follow these steps:

• Step 1: Visit the official website of the province or territory that you are interested in. You need to visit the official website of the province or territory that you want to immigrate to and find the section that explains their PNP and its streams. You will find information about the eligibility criteria, requirements, application process, fees, processing times, etc. of each PNP stream. You will also find links to online application forms and portals that you can use to apply for a provincial nomination.

• Step 2: Choose the PNP stream that suits you best. You need to choose the PNP stream that matches your skills, education, work experience, language ability, job offer, connection to the province or territory, etc. You also need to make sure that you meet the minimum criteria and requirements of the PNP stream that you choose. You can use the online tools and checklists that some provinces or territories provide to assess your eligibility and suitability for their PNP streams.

• Step 3: Create an online account and fill out your application form. You need to create an online account on the website of the province or territory that you are applying for. You will need an email address and a password to create your account. You will also need to answer some security questions and agree to some terms and conditions. Once you create your account, you can access and fill out your application form online. You will have to answer some questions about yourself and your family members, such as your personal details, education, work experience, language skills, job offer, connection to the province or territory, etc. You will have to provide accurate and complete information that matches your supporting documents.

• Step 4: Pay your application fees online. You need to pay your application fees online using your online account. The application fees vary depending on the province or territory and the PNP stream that you are applying for, but they usually range from $100 CAD to $2,000 CAD per person. You can pay your fees by credit card, debit card, or prepaid card.

• Step 5: Upload your supporting documents online. You need to upload your supporting documents online using your online account. The supporting documents include proof of identity, proof of education, proof of work experience, proof of language skills, proof of funds, proof of medical exams, proof of police certificates, proof of job offer or provincial nomination (if applicable), etc. You will also have to provide translations and certifications for any documents that are not in English or French. You will have to follow the specific format and size requirements that the province or territory provides for each document.

How to apply for a provincial nomination through a PNP stream by mail?

To apply for a provincial nomination through a PNP stream by mail, you need to follow these steps:

• Step 1: Visit the official website of the province or territory that you are interested in. You need to visit the official website of the province or territory that you want to immigrate to and find the section that explains their PNP and its streams. You will find information about the eligibility criteria, requirements, application process, fees, processing times, etc. of each PNP stream. You will also find links to download the application forms and guides that you can use to apply for a provincial nomination.

• Step 2: Choose the PNP stream that suits you best. You need to choose the PNP stream that matches your skills, education, work experience, language ability, job offer, connection to the province or territory, etc. You also need to make sure that you meet the minimum criteria and requirements of the PNP stream that you choose. You can use the online tools and checklists that some provinces or territories provide to assess your eligibility and suitability for their PNP streams.

• Step 3: Print and fill out your application form by hand or by computer. You need to print and fill out your application form by hand or by computer using the application guide that the province or territory provides. You will have to answer some questions about yourself and your family members, such as your personal details, education, work experience, language skills, job offer, connection to the province or territory, etc. You will have to provide accurate and complete information that matches your supporting documents.

- Step 4: Pay your application fees by cheque or money order. You need to pay your application fees by cheque or money order made payable to the province or territory that you are applying for. The application fees vary depending on the province or territory and the PNP stream that you are applying for, but they usually range from $100 CAD to $2,000 CAD per person. You will have to include your cheque or money order with your application form and supporting documents.

- Step 5: Gather and photocopy your supporting documents. You need to gather and photocopy your supporting documents that prove your identity, education, work experience, language skills, funds, medical exams, police certificates, job offer or provincial nomination (if applicable), etc. You will also have to provide translations and certifications for any documents that are not in English or French. You will have to follow the specific format and size requirements that the province or territory provides for each document.

These are the steps to apply for a provincial nomination through a PNP stream by mail or online. In the next subsection, I will explain how to apply for permanent residence after receiving a provincial nomination from a province or territory.

How to apply for permanent residence after receiving a provincial nomination from a province or territory?

If you receive a provincial nomination from a province or territory, you can apply for permanent residence through IRCC online or by mail. This is the final step of applying for Canadian immigration through the PNP.

What is a provincial nomination and how to accept it?

A provincial nomination is a certificate or letter that a province or territory issues to an immigrant who meets their specific economic and social needs. A provincial nomination means that the province or territory has selected you to immigrate to their region. A provincial nomination also gives you 600 additional points in your CRS score, which virtually guarantees that you will receive an ITA from IRCC.

To accept your provincial nomination, you need to follow these steps:

• Step 1: Log in to your online account on the website of the province or territory that nominated you. You need to log in to your online account where you can access and manage your PNP application and nomination. You will see a notification that you have received a provincial nomination from the province or territory.

• Step 2: Confirm your interest in immigrating to the province or territory that nominated you. You need to confirm that you are interested in immigrating to the province or territory that nominated you. You will have to answer some questions about your personal information, such as your name, date of birth, passport number, etc. You will also have to agree to some terms and conditions.

• Step 3: Receive your nomination certificate or letter from the province or territory that nominated you. Once you confirm your interest in immigrating to the province or territory that nominated you, they will send you a nomination certificate or letter by email or mail. This document will contain your personal information, your nomination details, and your nomination number.

These are the steps to accept your provincial nomination from a province or territory. You will have 30 days from the date of your provincial nomination to apply for permanent residence through IRCC online or by mail. If you do not accept your provincial nomination or apply for permanent residence within 30 days, your provincial nomination will expire, and you will lose your chance to immigrate to Canada. You will also have to re-apply for a provincial nomination through the PNP stream that you applied for.

How to apply for permanent residence through IRCC online or by mail after receiving a provincial nomination?

To apply for permanent residence through IRCC online or by mail after receiving a provincial nomination, you need to follow these steps:

• Step 1: Visit the official website of IRCC and find the section that explains how to apply for permanent residence as a provincial nominee. You need to visit the official website of IRCC and find the section that explains how to apply for permanent residence as a provincial nominee. You will find information about the eligibility criteria, requirements, application process, fees, processing times, etc. of applying for permanent residence as a provincial nominee. You will also find links to download the application forms and guides that you can use to apply for permanent residence as a provincial nominee.

• Step 2: Choose whether you want to apply online or by mail. You need to choose whether you want to apply online or by mail depending on your preference and convenience. Applying online is faster and easier than applying by mail, but it requires having access to a computer and an internet connection. Applying by mail is slower and more complicated than applying online, but it does not require having access to a computer and an internet connection.

• Step 3: Fill out your application forms online or by hand or by computer. You need to fill out your application forms online using your online account on IRCC's website if you choose to apply online, or by hand or by computer using the application guide that IRCC provides if you choose to apply by mail. You will have to answer some questions about yourself and your family members, such as your personal details, education, work experience, language skills, etc. You will also have to declare any changes or updates in your information since you received your provincial nomination. You will have to provide accurate and complete information that matches your supporting documents. If you provide false or misleading information, IRCC may refuse your application or ban you from applying for five years.

Section 4: Student Immigration

If you are a student who wants to pursue your education in Canada, you may be eligible for student immigration. Student immigration allows you to come to Canada with a study permit and access the high-quality and affordable education system. In this section, we will explain who is eligible for student immigration, what are the requirements, and how to apply.

Who is eligible for student immigration?

Student immigration is open to foreign nationals who want to study at a Canadian educational institution that is approved by the government. You can apply for student immigration if you:

• Have been accepted by a designated learning institution (DLI) in Canada

• Have enough money to pay for your tuition fees, living expenses, and return transportation.

• Have no criminal record and are not a security risk.

• Are in good health and willing to undergo a medical exam if required.

• Plan to leave Canada at the end of your authorized stay.

THE ULTIMATE GUIDE TO CANADIAN IMMIGRATION PATHWAYS

What are the requirements for student immigration?

The main requirement for student immigration is to obtain a study permit. A study permit is a document that allows you to enter and stay in Canada as a student. To get a study permit, you need to:

• Apply online or on paper to Immigration, Refugees and Citizenship Canada (IRCC) before you travel to Canada.

• Provide proof of your acceptance by a DLI in Canada

• Provide proof of your financial ability to cover your costs in Canada.

• Provide proof of your identity, such as a passport or travel document

• Provide proof of your language proficiency in English or French, such as a test result or a certificate

• Provide any other documents or information requested by IRCC, such as a letter of explanation, a custodian declaration (if you are a minor), or a biometric data (if applicable)

Depending on your country of origin, you may also need to obtain a temporary resident visa (TRV) or an electronic travel authorization (eTA) to enter Canada. A TRV is a sticker that is placed on your passport that shows that you have met the requirements to enter Canada as a visitor. An eTA is an electronic authorization that is linked to your passport that allows you to board a flight to Canada. You can check if you need a TRV or an eTA on the IRCC website.

How to apply for student immigration?

The application process for student immigration consists of the following steps:

• Step 1: Choose a DLI and a study program. You need to research the different DLIs and study programs in Canada and find the one that suits your needs and goals. You can use various sources of information, such as the official websites of the DLIs, online forums, blogs, or videos of other students who have studied in Canada, or professional advice from an education agent or consultant.

• Step 2: Apply for admission and get an acceptance letter. You need to apply for admission to the DLI and the study program of your choice. You need to meet the admission requirements and submit an application with all the required documents and fees. If your application is successful, you will receive an acceptance letter from the DLI that confirms your admission and provides details about your study program, such as the start date, end date, tuition fees, etc.

• Step 3: Apply for a study permit and a TRV or an eTA (if applicable). You need to apply for a study permit and a TRV or an eTA (if applicable) before you travel to Canada. You need to submit an application with all the required documents and fees. You can apply online through the IRCC website or on paper through a visa application centre (VAC) in your country. If your application is approved, you will receive a letter of introduction that shows that you have been approved for a study permit and a TRV or an eTA (if applicable) that allows you to enter Canada.

• Step 4: Travel to Canada and start your studies. You need to travel to Canada with your passport, letter of introduction, acceptance letter, TRV or eTA (if applicable), and any other documents or information that you may need to show at the port of entry. You need to present these documents to the border officer who will verify them and issue your study permit. You also need to comply with any conditions or restrictions that may be imposed on your study permit, such as reporting your arrival, enrolling in your DLI, working while studying, etc.

In summary, student immigration is an option for foreign nationals who want to study at a Canadian educational institution that is approved by the government. You can apply for student immigration by obtaining a study permit and a TRV or an eTA (if applicable) before you travel to Canada. You can also benefit from studying in Canada by accessing high-quality and affordable education, gaining valuable skills and experience, working while studying or after graduation, and applying for permanent residence.

In Section 3, we will explore another option for immigrating to Canada: family sponsorship immigration. We will explain who is eligible for family sponsorship immigration, what are the requirements, and how to apply.

Chapter 2: Exploring Other Canadian Immigration Pathways

Section 1: Family Sponsorship Immigration

IF YOU HAVE A FAMILY member who is a Canadian citizen or a permanent resident, you may be eligible for family sponsorship immigration. Family sponsorship immigration allows you to join your relatives in Canada and become a permanent resident yourself. In this section, we will explain who is eligible for family sponsorship immigration, what are the requirements, and how to apply.

Who is eligible for family sponsorship immigration?

Family sponsorship immigration is open to foreign nationals who are related to a Canadian citizen or a permanent resident who is willing and able to sponsor them. You can apply for family sponsorship immigration if you are one of the following:

• Spouse or common-law partner: You are married to or living in a conjugal relationship with your sponsor for at least one year. You must prove that your relationship is genuine and not entered into for immigration purposes.

• Dependent child: You are the biological or adopted child of your sponsor or their spouse or partner. You must be under 22 years old and not married or in a common-law relationship. If you are over 22 years old, you must have depended on your sponsor financially since before you turned 22 and be unable to support yourself due to a physical or mental condition.

• Parent or grandparent: You are the parent or grandparent of your sponsor or their spouse or partner. You must be sponsored under the Parents and Grandparents Program (PGP), which has a limited number of applications each year. You must also meet the income requirement of your sponsor and sign an undertaking to repay any social assistance that you may receive from the government.

• Other relative: You are the brother, sister, nephew, niece, grandchild, uncle, aunt, or other relative of your sponsor or their spouse or partner. You can only be sponsored under this category if your sponsor does not have any other relatives who are eligible for family sponsorship immigration and does not have any relatives who are Canadian citizens or permanent residents.

What are the requirements for family sponsorship immigration?

The main requirement for family sponsorship immigration is to have a sponsor who is a Canadian citizen or a permanent resident who is at least 18 years old and lives in Canada. Your sponsor must:

• Apply to become your sponsor and agree to support you financially for a certain period of time.

• Meet the income requirement for sponsoring parents and grandparents (if applicable)

• Sign an undertaking to repay any social assistance that you may receive from the government.

• Not be inadmissible to Canada for criminal, security, medical, or other reasons.

• Not be in default of any previous sponsorship undertaking, immigration loan, court order, or support payment.

You, as the person being sponsored, must also:

• Apply to become a permanent resident and agree to live in Canada.

• Meet the eligibility criteria and requirements of the family class that you belong to

• Not be inadmissible to Canada for criminal, security, medical, or other reasons.

• Submit an application with all the required documents and fees.

How to apply for family sponsorship immigration?

The application process for family sponsorship immigration consists of two parts:

• Part 1: Your sponsor applies to become your sponsor. Your sponsor must download and complete the PDF forms in the application package on the IRCC website. Your sponsor must also digitally sign the forms along with you (the principal applicant) and any other family members included in the application. Your sponsor must then upload the forms to their online application portal account and electronically sign for the entire application. Your sponsor must also pay the sponsorship fee, the processing fee, and the right of permanent residence fee (if applicable).

• Part 2: You apply to become a permanent resident. You must fill out these digital forms online:

o Generic Application Form for Canada (IMM 0008)

o Schedule A – Background/Declaration (IMM 5669)

o Additional Family Information (IMM 5406)

o Supplementary Information - Your travels (IMM 5562)

You must also scan and upload both sides of your photo according to the photo specifications. You must then submit your online application through your permanent residence online application portal account. You must also pay the biometric fee (if applicable).

Depending on your country of origin, you may also need to obtain a temporary resident visa (TRV) or an electronic travel authorization (eTA) to enter Canada. A TRV is a sticker that is placed on your passport that shows that you have met the requirements to enter Canada as a visitor. An eTA is an electronic authorization that is linked to your passport that allows you to board a flight to Canada. You can check if you need a TRV or an eTA on the IRCC website.

In summary, family sponsorship immigration is an option for foreign nationals who have a relative who is a Canadian citizen or a permanent resident who is willing and able to sponsor them. You can apply for family sponsorship immigration by having your sponsor apply to become your sponsor and by applying to become a permanent resident yourself. You can also benefit from family sponsorship immigration by reuniting with your loved ones, accessing social services and benefits, and applying for Canadian citizenship.

Section 2: The Business Immigration Programs

If you are a business person who wants to come to Canada and start, buy, or invest in a business, you may be interested in the business immigration programs. These are special immigration programs that allow you to apply for permanent residence based on your business skills, experience, and contribution to the Canadian economy. In this section, we will explain what are the business immigration programs and how they work, what are the eligibility criteria and requirements for the different programs, how to apply for a program based on your business plan, net worth, investment amount, and how to apply for permanent residence after being approved for a program.

What are the business immigration programs and how they work

The business immigration programs are part of Canada's economic immigration system. They aim to attract entrepreneurs, investors, and self-employed persons who can create jobs, stimulate innovation, and enhance competitiveness in Canada. There are different types of business immigration programs, each with its own objectives, criteria, and processes. Some of the main business immigration programs are:

• **Start-up Visa Program**: This program is for innovative entrepreneurs who have a qualifying business idea and a letter of support from a designated organization in Canada. A designated organization is a group that has been approved by the government to invest in or support start-up businesses. These can be angel investors, venture capital funds, or business incubators. The Start-up Visa Program allows you to apply for permanent residence if you meet the following requirements:

o You have a qualifying business that is incorporated in Canada and has at least 10% of the voting rights attached to all shares.

o You have a letter of support from one or more designated organizations that confirm they will invest or support your business.

o You have enough money to settle and live in Canada.

o You have at least one year of post-secondary education

o You have a minimum level of proficiency in English or French

o You meet the health and security requirements

• **Self-Employed Persons Program**: This program is for individuals who have relevant experience and can create their own employment by contributing to Canada's cultural or athletic life. This can include artists, writers, musicians, athletes, coaches, trainers, etc. The Self-Employed Persons Program allows you to apply for permanent residence if you meet the following requirements:

o You have at least two years of relevant experience in cultural or athletic activities at a world-class level or being self-employed in such activities

o You have the intention and ability to create your own employment in Canada in your field of expertise

o You have enough money to settle and live in Canada

o You meet the health and security requirements

THE ULTIMATE GUIDE TO CANADIAN IMMIGRATION PATHWAYS

- **Entrepreneur Program**: This program is for experienced business owners or managers who want to establish or acquire a business in Canada that will create jobs and economic growth. This program is only available through some provincial nominee programs (PNPs), which are immigration programs that allow provinces and territories to nominate candidates for permanent residence based on their specific needs. The Entrepreneur Program allows you to apply for permanent residence if you meet the following requirements:

  o You have a minimum net worth of $300,000 CAD (or more depending on the province)

  o You have at least three years of experience in owning or managing a qualifying business.

  o You have a viable business plan that meets the criteria of the province where you intend to operate your business.

  o You make a minimum investment of $150,000 CAD (or more depending on the province) in your business.

  o You create at least one full-time job for a Canadian citizen or permanent resident (other than yourself or your family members)

  o You meet the language, education, health and security requirements

- **Investor Program**: This program is for individuals who have a high net worth and want to make a significant investment in Canada's economy. This program is also only available through some provincial nominee programs (PNPs). The Investor Program allows you to apply for permanent residence if you meet the following requirements:

o You have a minimum net worth of $800,000 CAD (or more depending on the province)

o You have at least five years of experience in owning or managing a qualifying business or working in a senior management role.

o You make a minimum investment of $200,000 CAD (or more depending on the province) in an approved fund that supports economic development and innovation in Canada.

o You meet the language, education, health and security requirements

These are some of the main business immigration programs that Canada offers. There may be other programs or streams that suit your specific situation better. For example, some provinces have special programs for farmers, community supporters, international graduates, etc. You can check the websites of each province or territory to find out more about their business immigration options.

How to apply for a business immigration program based on your business plan, net worth, investment amount, etc.

The application process for a business immigration program depends on the type of program you choose and the province where you want to operate your business. However, there are some common steps that you need to follow:

• **Do your research**: Before you apply for a business immigration program, you need to do your research and find out which program is best suited for your goals, skills, and resources. You need to compare the different programs and their requirements, benefits, and challenges.

You also need to research the market conditions, opportunities, and regulations in the province where you want to start or buy your business. You can use online tools such as the Business Immigration Tool or the Business Immigration Explorer to help you find the right program and province for you.

• **Prepare your documents**: Once you have decided on a program and a province, you need to prepare your documents for your application. You will need to provide proof of your identity, status, education, work experience, language ability, funds, net worth, investment amount, business plan, etc. You may also need to obtain a medical exam report and a police certificate. You should follow the instructions and checklist provided by the program or province that you are applying to. Make sure your documents are clear, complete, accurate, and valid.

• **Submit your application**: Depending on the program and province that you are applying to, you may need to submit your application online or by mail. You will also need to pay the application fees. You will receive a confirmation number and an email notification once your application is received. You should keep track of your application status and respond to any requests or updates from the immigration authorities.

• **Wait for a decision**: The processing time for a business immigration application varies depending on the program and province that you are applying to. There is no guarantee that your application will be approved. The immigration authorities will assess your application based on the information and evidence you provide, as well as other factors such as the economic impact, innovation potential, job creation potential, and viability of your business. You may be asked to provide additional information or attend an interview during the process. If your application is approved, you will receive a letter of approval or a nomination certificate from the program or province that you applied to.

How to apply for permanent residence after being approved for a business immigration program.

After you have been approved for a business immigration program, you can apply for permanent residence in Canada. The process for applying for permanent residence depends on whether you applied through a federal or a provincial program.

• **If you applied through a federal program**: If you applied through the Start-up Visa Program or the Self-Employed Persons Program, you can apply for permanent residence online through the Permanent Residence Online Application Portal. You will need to create an account, fill out the application forms, upload your documents, pay the fees, and submit your application. You will receive a confirmation number and an email notification once your application is received.

• **If you applied through a provincial program**: If you applied through a provincial nominee program (PNP), such as the Entrepreneur Program or the Investor Program, you would need to apply for permanent residence in two stages. First, you will need to apply to the province where you want to operate your business and get nominated by them. Second, you will need to apply to Immigration, Refugees and Citizenship Canada (IRCC) and get approved by them. You can apply online through Express Entry or by paper depending on the stream that you are nominated under.

We hope this section helps you understand how to apply for permanent residence through the business immigration programs. If you have any questions or need assistance with your application, please feel free to contact us at any time. We would be happy to guide you through this process and help you achieve your immigration goals.

Section 3: The Humanitarian and Compassionate Grounds Program

In this section, you will learn about another economic immigration program that is not managed by IRCC or provincial governments, but by other federal departments or agencies. This program is called the humanitarian and compassionate grounds program.

What is the humanitarian and compassionate grounds program and how does it works ?

The humanitarian and compassionate grounds program is a program that allows foreign nationals who are in Canada or outside Canada to apply for permanent residence based on their personal circumstances that make them eligible for special consideration from IRCC. The humanitarian and compassionate grounds program is designed to address the cases that do not fit into any other immigration category or program, but where there are compelling reasons to grant permanent residence to the applicants.

The humanitarian and compassionate grounds program works in one step:

• Step 1: Apply for permanent residence on humanitarian and compassionate grounds. You need to submit an application for permanent residence on humanitarian and compassionate grounds to IRCC online or by mail. You will have to fill out some application forms and pay some application fees. You will also have to submit some supporting documents, such as proof of identity, proof of education, proof of work experience, proof of language skills, proof of funds, proof of medical exams, proof of police certificates, etc. You will also have to provide a detailed explanation of your personal circumstances that make you eligible for humanitarian and compassionate consideration from IRCC.

Next up, I will explain the eligibility criteria and requirements for applying on humanitarian and compassionate grounds.

What are the eligibility criteria and requirements for applying on humanitarian and compassionate grounds?

To be eligible for applying on humanitarian and compassionate grounds, you need to meet the following criteria:

• You need to be a foreign national who is in Canada or outside Canada. If you are in Canada, you need to have a valid temporary status or be eligible to restore your status. If you are outside Canada, you need to have a strong connection to Canada or face exceptional hardship in your country of origin.

• You need to have personal circumstances that make you eligible for humanitarian and compassionate consideration from IRCC. These circumstances may include factors such as your establishment in Canada, your family ties in Canada, the best interests of any children affected by your application, the consequences of your separation from your relatives, the conditions in your country of origin, the impact of your removal from Canada, etc.

• You need to demonstrate that you would face unusual, undeserved, or disproportionate hardship if you are not granted permanent residence. This means that you would face more than the normal difficulties or disadvantages that most people face when they leave their country of origin or return to it.

• You need to show that you have made efforts to regularize your immigration status through other means before applying on humanitarian and compassionate grounds. This means that you have explored and exhausted all the possible options to apply for permanent residence through other immigration categories or programs, such as family sponsorship, economic immigration, refugee protection, etc.

These are the eligibility criteria for applying on humanitarian and compassionate grounds. However, meeting these criteria does not guarantee that you will be approved for permanent residence on humanitarian and compassionate grounds. You will still have to compete with other applicants on humanitarian and compassionate grounds and meet the federal admissibility requirements. Therefore, it is important to prepare and submit your application carefully and convincingly.

Next, I will let you know how to demonstrate your exceptional circumstances that warrant special consideration from IRCC. Let's go!

How to demonstrate your exceptional circumstances that warrant special consideration from IRCC?

To demonstrate your exceptional circumstances that warrant special consideration from IRCC, you need to provide a detailed explanation of your personal situation and how it affects you and your family members. You need to show that you have compelling reasons to stay in Canada or come to Canada and that you would face unusual, undeserved, or disproportionate hardship if you are not granted permanent residence. You also need to provide evidence to support your claims and arguments.

Some of the factors that you can use to demonstrate your exceptional circumstances are:

● Your establishment in Canada: This refers to the extent and quality of your social, economic, and cultural integration in Canada. You can show how long you have been living in Canada, what activities and contributions you have made to your community, what ties and relationships you have with Canadians, what skills and qualifications you have acquired or improved in Canada, etc.

• Your family ties in Canada: This refers to the impact of your separation from your relatives who are in Canada or who depend on you. You can show how close and important your family relationships are, what roles and responsibilities you have within your family, what emotional and financial support you provide or receive from your family, what hardships or risks your family would face if you leave Canada or cannot come to Canada, etc.

• The best interests of any children affected by your application: This refers to the well-being and welfare of any children who are involved in your application, either as applicants or as dependents. You can show how your immigration status affects the children's physical, mental, emotional, and educational development, what opportunities and challenges the children have in Canada or in your country of origin, what preferences and opinions the children have regarding their immigration situation, etc.

• The conditions in your country of origin: This refers to the situation and circumstances that you face or would face in your country of origin. You can show how safe or unsafe your country of origin is, what human rights violations or abuses you have experienced or would experience in your country of origin, what social or economic difficulties or disadvantages you have encountered or would encounter in your country of origin, etc.

• The impact of your removal from Canada: This refers to the consequences and implications of leaving Canada permanently or temporarily. You can show how difficult or impossible it would be for you to return to Canada legally or illegally, what barriers or obstacles you would face in re-establishing yourself in Canada or in another country, what losses or damages you would suffer as a result of leaving Canada, etc.

These are some of the factors that you can use to demonstrate your exceptional circumstances that warrant special consideration from IRCC. However, these factors are not exhaustive or definitive. You may have other factors that are relevant and important for your case. You need to explain and justify why these factors make you eligible for humanitarian and compassionate consideration from IRCC.

To provide evidence for these factors, you need to submit some supporting documents with your application. These documents may include letters, affidavits, testimonials, reports, certificates, records, etc. that verify and corroborate your claims and arguments. You also need to provide translations and certifications for any documents that are not in English or French.

Next up, I will show you how to apply for permanent residence on humanitarian and compassionate grounds. Let's go!

How To Apply for Permanent Residence on Humanitarian and Compassionate Grounds

To apply for permanent residence on humanitarian and compassionate grounds. Here are the steps you need to follow:

- Determine if you are eligible to apply. You can use this application if you are in Canada, and you need an exemption from one or more requirements of the Immigration and Refugee Protection Act or Regulations in order to apply for permanent residence within Canada. You also need to show that you would face unusual, undeserved, or disproportionate hardship if you had to leave Canada. You cannot apply if you are eligible for any of these classes: Spouse or Common-Law Partner, Live-in Caregiver, Caregivers: caring for children or people with high medical needs, Protected Person and Convention Refugees, and Temporary Resident Permit Holder.

- Gather the required documents. You will need to fill out two forms: the Generic Application Form for Canada (IMM 0008), and the Schedule A – Background/Declaration (IMM 5669). You will also need to provide proof of your identity, such as a passport or travel document, proof of your status in Canada, such as a visitor visa or work permit, proof of your income and expenses, such as tax returns or bank statements, proof of your ties to Canada, such as family members, friends, community involvement, or education, proof of the hardship you would face if you had to leave Canada, such as medical reports, letters of support, or country conditions reports. You may also need to provide other documents depending on your situation, such as police certificates, language test results, or biometrics.

- Pay the application fees. You will need to pay the processing fee and the right of permanent residence fee for yourself, and each family member included in your application. The processing fee is $550 CAD per person, and the right of permanent residence fee is $500 CAD per person. You can pay online using a credit card or a prepaid card. If you cannot afford to pay the fees, you can request a fee waiver by filling out the Request for a Fee Waiver (IMM 5783) form and providing evidence of your financial hardship[12].

- Submit your application online. You can apply online

through the Permanent Residence Online Application Portal[12]. You will need to create an account, upload your forms and documents, pay your fees, and submit your application. You will receive a confirmation number and an email notification once your application is received.

- Wait for a decision on your application. The processing time for humanitarian and compassionate applications varies depending on the complexity of your case and the volume of applications received by Immigration, Refugees and Citizenship Canada (IRCC). There is no guarantee that your application will be approved. IRCC will assess your application based on the information and evidence you provide, as well as other factors such as the best interests of any children involved, public policy considerations, international obligations, and security and criminality checks. You may be asked to provide additional information or attend an interview during the process[12]. If your application is approved, you will be granted permanent resident status and receive a confirmation of permanent residence document. If your application is refused, you will receive a letter explaining the reasons for the refusal and your options to appeal or reapply.

Section 4: The Atlantic Immigration Pilot Program (AIPP)

This is another economic immigration program that is not managed by IRCC or provincial governments. This program is called the Atlantic Immigration Pilot Program (AIPP).

What is the AIPP and how does it work?

The AIPP is a program that allows employers in the four Atlantic provinces of Canada (New Brunswick, Newfoundland and Labrador, Nova Scotia, and Prince Edward Island) to hire foreign workers who can fill their labour shortages and contribute to their economic growth. The AIPP is designed to address the specific challenges and opportunities that these provinces face, such as aging population, low immigration rates, skills gaps, etc. The AIPP also gives immigrants more options and flexibility to choose where they want to live and work in Canada.

The AIPP has three steps: getting a job offer, getting your documents ready, and applying for permanent residence. In this guide, we will explain each step in more detail and provide you with some tips and resources to help you succeed in each step.

Step 1: Getting a job offer.

The first step of the AIPP is to get a job offer from a designated employer in Atlantic Canada. A designated employer is an employer who has been approved by the provincial government to participate in the program1. You can find a list of designated employers on the websites of each province. You can also use the Job Bank website to search for jobs that are eligible for the AIPP.

To get a job offer, you need to contact employers directly and show them that you have the skills and qualifications they are looking for. You can use your resume, cover letter, portfolio, references, or any other documents that demonstrate your abilities and achievements. You can also use online platforms such as LinkedIn or Indeed to network with employers and showcase your profile.

Some tips for getting a job offer are:

• Do your research. Learn about the employer, the industry, and the region before you apply. Find out what their needs, challenges, and goals are, and how you can help them achieve them.

• Tailor your application. Customize your resume and cover letter to match the specific requirements and expectations of the job. Highlight your relevant skills, experience, and achievements, and use keywords from the job posting.

• Follow up. After you apply, send a follow-up email or call the employer to express your interest and enthusiasm for the job. Ask if they have any questions or need any additional information from you.

• Prepare for the interview. If you are invited for an interview, prepare yourself by reviewing your resume, researching common interview questions, and practicing your answers. Dress professionally, be punctual, and be confident.

If you receive a job offer from a designated employer, make sure that it meets the following criteria:

• It is full-time and non-seasonal (at least 30 hours per week)

• It is for at least one year

- It is in a skilled occupation (National Occupational Classification skill level 0, A, B or C)

- It meets or exceeds the provincial minimum wage

The employer will also need to provide you with a settlement plan that outlines the support and services they will offer you to help you adjust to life in Canada. The settlement plan will include information on topics such as housing, transportation, health care, education, language training, banking, and community resources.

Step 2: Getting your documents ready.

The second step of the AIPP is to get your documents ready for your permanent residence application. You will need to provide proof of your identity, status, education, work experience, language ability, funds, and medical exam. You will also need to obtain a certificate of endorsement from the province where you will be working.

Some of the documents you will need are:

- Passport or travel document

- Birth certificate or other proof of identity

- Work permit or other proof of status in Canada (if applicable)

- Educational credential assessment (ECA) report (if you have a foreign degree, diploma or certificate)

- Proof of work experience (such as letters of reference from employers or pay stubs)

- Language test results (such as IELTS or CELPIP for English or TEF or TCF for French)

- Proof of funds (such as bank statements or letters from financial institutions)

- Medical exam report (from a panel physician approved by IRCC)

- Certificate of endorsement (from the provincial government)

Some tips for getting your documents ready are:

- Start early. Some documents may take time to obtain or process, so start collecting them as soon as possible. Check the expiry dates of your documents and make sure they are valid at the time of your application.

- Follow the instructions. Read the document checklist carefully and follow the instructions on how to obtain, format, scan, upload, and submit your documents. Make sure your documents are clear, legible, complete, and accurate.

- Keep copies. Keep copies of all your documents for your own records. You may need them later for verification or confirmation purposes.

Step 3: Applying for permanent residence.

The third step of the AIPP is to apply for permanent residence online through the Permanent Residence Online Application Portal1. You will need to create an account, fill out the application forms, upload your documents, pay the application fees, and submit your application. You will receive a confirmation number and an email notification once your application is received.

Some of the application forms you will need to fill out are:

- Generic Application Form for Canada (IMM 0008)

- Schedule A – Background/Declaration (IMM 5669)

• Additional Family Information (IMM 5406)

• Schedule 4 – Economic Classes: Atlantic Immigration Pilot Program (IMM 0008 SCHEDULE 4)

Some of the application fees you will need to pay are:

• Processing fee ($550 CAD per person)

• Right of permanent residence fee ($500 CAD per person)

• Biometrics fee ($85 CAD per person or $170 CAD per family)

Some tips for applying for permanent residence are:

• Be honest. Provide truthful and accurate information in your application. Do not omit, falsify, or misrepresent any facts or documents. If you do, your application may be refused or you may be banned from applying for immigration for five years.

• Be consistent. Make sure the information you provide in your application matches the information in your documents. If there are any discrepancies or changes, explain them clearly and provide supporting evidence.

• Be responsive. Check your email regularly for any updates or requests from IRCC. Respond to them as soon as possible and provide any additional information or documents they ask for.

After you apply, you will need to wait for a decision on your application. The processing time for AIPP applications varies depending on the complexity of your case and the volume of applications received by IRCC. There is no guarantee that your application will be approved. IRCC will assess your application based on the information and evidence you provide, as well as other factors such as the best interests of any children involved, public policy considerations, international obligations, and security and criminality checks.

If your application is approved, you will be granted permanent resident status and receive a confirmation of permanent residence document. You will also receive instructions on how to complete your landing process and receive your permanent resident card.

If your application is refused, you will receive a letter explaining the reasons for the refusal and your options to appeal or reapply.

Chapter 3: Preparing Your Immigration Application

IN CHAPTER 2, WE EXPLORED your immigration options based on your skills, education, work experience, and family situation. In this Chapter, we will explain how to prepare your immigration application, including gathering your documents, completing your forms, and paying your fees.

Section 1: Gathering Your Documents

One of the most important steps in preparing your immigration application is to gather your documents. Your documents are the evidence that you provide to support your application and prove your identity, eligibility, and suitability for immigration to Canada. In this section, we will explain what types of documents you need to prepare, how to obtain, translate, and certify them, and how to organize them.

What types of documents do you need to prepare?

The types of documents that you need to prepare depend on the program or stream that you apply under, the country or territory that you are applying from, and your personal situation. However, some common types of documents that apply to most immigration applications are:

• Identity documents: These are documents that show your name, date of birth, place of birth, citizenship, and other personal information. Examples of identity documents are passport, birth certificate, national identity card, etc.

- Education documents: These are documents that show your level of education, qualifications, and credentials. Examples of education documents are diploma, degree, transcript, educational credential assessment (ECA) report, etc.

- Work documents: These are documents that show your work experience, skills, and occupation. Examples of work documents are employment letters, pay stubs, tax returns, reference letters, etc.

- Language test results: These are documents that show your proficiency in English or French. Examples of language test results are International English Language Testing System (IELTS), Canadian English Language Proficiency Index Program (CELPIP), Test d'évaluation de français (TEF), etc.

- Medical exam results: These are documents that show that you have undergone a medical exam by a panel physician approved by the Canadian government and that you do not have any health condition that may pose a danger to public health or safety or cause excessive demand on health or social services in Canada.

- Police certificates: These are documents that show that you have no criminal record or pending charges in any country or territory that you have lived in for six months or more since you turned 18 years old.

- Other documents: These are documents that may be required depending on your situation or the program or stream that you apply under. Examples of other documents are marriage certificate, divorce certificate, death certificate, adoption certificate, custody agreement, proof of funds, job offer letter, provincial nomination certificate, letter of explanation, etc.

THE ULTIMATE GUIDE TO CANADIAN IMMIGRATION PATHWAYS

You can find the list of specific documents that you need to prepare for your immigration application on the IRCC website or in the document checklist that is included in the application package.

How to obtain, translate, and certify your documents?

You need to obtain original or certified copies of your documents from the official authorities or institutions that issued them. You also need to make sure that your documents are valid and up-to-date at the time of your application.

If your documents are not in English or French, you need to translate them into one of these official languages. You also need to provide a copy of the original document and a signed declaration from the translator stating their name, contact information, and language proficiency. The translator must be certified by a regulatory body or have a seal from a professional association. You can find a list of certified translators on the IRCC website.

If your documents are not issued by a Canadian authority or institution, you may need to certify them according to the Canadian immigration standards. This means that you need to have an authorized person make a copy of your original document and sign and stamp it with their name, title, contact information, and statement confirming its authenticity. The authorized person must be someone who has the legal authority to certify documents in your country or territory. You can find a list of authorized persons on the IRCC website.

How to organize your documents?

You need to organize your documents according to the order and format specified by IRCC. You also need to label each document clearly with its name and number. You can use the document checklist as a guide for organizing your documents.

If you apply online through Express Entry or another online portal, you need to scan and upload your documents as PDF files. You also need to make sure that each file is less than 4 MB in size and has a clear resolution and quality.

If you apply on paper through a visa application centre (VAC) or another office, you need to print and submit two copies of each document. You also need to make sure that each copy is clear and legible and has no staples or paper clips.

In summary, gathering your documents is an essential step in preparing your immigration application. You need to prepare the types of documents that match your program or stream and situation. You also need to obtain original or certified copies, translate them into English or French, certify them according to Canadian standards, and organize them according to IRCC instructions.

In Section 2, we will explain another step in preparing your immigration application: completing your forms. We will explain what types of forms you need to complete, how to fill them out accurately and completely, and how to avoid common mistakes or inconsistencies.

Section 2: Completing Your Forms

Another important step in preparing your immigration application is to complete your forms. Your forms are the official documents that you use to provide information about yourself, your family members, your background, your eligibility, and your suitability for immigration to Canada. In this section, we will explain what types of forms you need to complete, how to fill them out accurately and completely, and how to avoid common mistakes or inconsistencies.

What types of forms do you need to complete?

The types of forms that you need to complete depend on the program or stream that you apply under, the country or territory that you are applying from, and your personal situation. However, some common types of forms that apply to most immigration applications are:

• Generic Application Form for Canada (IMM 0008): This is the main form that you use to apply for permanent residence in Canada. It contains information about yourself and your family members, such as your name, date of birth, place of birth, citizenship, marital status, education, work experience, etc.

• Schedule A – Background/Declaration (IMM 5669): This is a supplementary form that you use to provide more details about your background and declaration. It contains information about your personal history, such as your travel history, military service, membership in organizations, criminal record, etc.

• Additional Family Information (IMM 5406): This is another supplementary form that you use to provide more details about your family members. It contains information about your spouse or partner, your parents, your siblings, and your children, such as their name, date of birth, place of birth, citizenship, marital status, occupation, etc.

• Supplementary Information - Your travels (IMM 5562): This is an optional form that you use to provide more details about your travel history. It contains information about the countries or territories that you have visited or lived in for more than six months in the past 10 years.

You can find the list of specific forms that you need to complete for your immigration application on the IRCC website or in the document checklist that is included in the application package.

***

How to fill out your forms accurately and completely?

You need to fill out your forms accurately and completely according to the instructions provided by IRCC. You also need to make sure that your forms are consistent and compatible with each other and with your documents. Here are some tips and best practices for filling out your forms:

• Use a computer or a typewriter to fill out your forms. Do not use a pen or a pencil. If you need to make corrections, do not use white-out or cross-out. Instead, print a new form and start over.

• Use black ink only. Do not use any other color or highlighter.

• Use capital letters only. Do not use lower case letters or cursive writing.

• Use English or French only. Do not use any other language or alphabet.

• Use the exact same spelling and format for your name and other personal information as it appears on your passport or travel document. Do not use any abbreviations, nicknames, initials, or titles.

• Answer all the questions on the forms. Do not leave any blanks or write "N/A" (not applicable) or "NIL" (nothing). If a question does not apply to you or you do not know the answer, write "NONE" or "UNKNOWN".

• Provide accurate and truthful information on the forms. Do not lie, omit, or falsify any information. If you do so, you may face serious consequences, such as refusal, cancellation, revocation, removal, or criminal charges.

• Sign and date the forms where indicated. Do not sign for anyone else or use a stamp or a seal. If you are under 18 years old or have a legal guardian, your parent or guardian must sign for you.

How to avoid common mistakes or inconsistencies on your forms?

You need to avoid common mistakes or inconsistencies on your forms that may cause confusion, suspicion, or delay in the processing of your application. Here are some examples of common mistakes or inconsistencies that you should avoid:

• Providing incomplete or outdated information on your forms. For example, if you change your address, phone number, email address, marital status, occupation, etc., you should update your forms accordingly.

• Providing conflicting or contradictory information on different forms or documents. For example, if you state different dates of birth, places of birth, names of family members, etc., on different forms or documents, you should explain the reason for the discrepancy.

• Providing irrelevant or unnecessary information on your forms. For example, if you provide information that is not asked for or not related to the purpose of your application, such as your hobbies, interests, opinions, etc., you should delete it.

• Providing illegible or unclear information on your forms. For example, if you write in a way that is hard to read or understand, such as using poor handwriting, spelling errors, grammar errors, etc., you should correct it.

In summary, completing your forms is a crucial step in preparing your immigration application. You need to complete the types of forms that match your program or stream and situation. You also need to fill out your forms accurately and completely, and avoid common mistakes or inconsistencies.

In Section 3, we will explain the final step in preparing your immigration application: paying your fees. We will explain what types of fees you need to pay, how to pay them, and how to save money and avoid unnecessary or extra fees.

Section 3: Paying Your Fees

The final step in preparing your immigration application is to pay your fees. Your fees are the amount of money that you need to pay to the Canadian government for processing your application and providing you with immigration services. In this section, we will explain what types of fees you need to pay, how to pay them, and how to save money and avoid unnecessary or extra fees.

What types of fees do you need to pay?

The types of fees that you need to pay depend on the program or stream that you apply under, the country or territory that you are applying from, and your personal situation. However, some common types of fees that apply to most immigration applications are:

• Processing fee: This is the fee that you pay for the processing of your application for permanent residence. It covers the cost of verifying your information and documents, assessing your eligibility and suitability, and making a decision on your application. The processing fee varies depending on the program or stream that you apply under and the number of people included in your application. For example, if you apply as a skilled worker through Express Entry, the processing fee is $825 CAD per person.

• Right of permanent residence fee (RPRF): This is the fee that you pay for acquiring the right of permanent residence in Canada. It covers the cost of issuing your confirmation of permanent residence (COPR) and visa (if applicable) and registering you as a permanent resident. The RPRF is $500 CAD per person. You can pay this fee at the same time as your processing fee or later when you are approved for permanent residence.

• Biometric fee: This is the fee that you pay for providing your biometric data (fingerprints and photo) as part of your application. It covers the cost of collecting, storing, and verifying your biometric data. The biometric fee is $85 CAD per person or $170 CAD per family. You need to pay this fee if you are from a country or territory that requires biometrics to enter Canada.

• Other fees: These are fees that you may need to pay for other services or products related to your application, such as language tests, educational credential assessments (ECAs), medical exams, police certificates, translations, certifications, courier services, etc. These fees are not paid to the Canadian government but to the third-party providers that offer these services or products.

You can find the list of specific fees that you need to pay for your immigration application on the IRCC website or in the document checklist that is included in the application package.

How to pay your fees?

You need to pay your fees according to the methods and instructions provided by IRCC. You also need to make sure that your fees are paid in full and on time.

If you apply online through Express Entry or another online portal, you need to:

• Pay your fees online using a valid credit card or debit card.

• Print or save a copy of your receipt as proof of payment.

• Upload your receipt along with your other documents when you submit your online application.

If you apply on paper through a visa application centre (VAC) or another office, you need to:

• Pay your fees online using a valid credit card or debit card.

• Print or save a copy of your receipt as proof of payment.

• Include your receipt along with your other documents when you submit your paper-based application.

How to save money and avoid unnecessary or extra fees?

You can save money and avoid unnecessary or extra fees by following these tips and best practices:

• Plan ahead and apply early. You can avoid paying extra fees for rush services, expedited processing, or urgent travel arrangements by planning ahead and applying early for your immigration application. You can also take advantage of lower fees or discounts offered by some service or product providers if you book or purchase in advance.

• Compare and choose wisely. You can save money by comparing and choosing wisely among the different service or product providers that offer language tests, ECAs, medical exams, police certificates, translations, certifications, courier services, etc. You can look for providers that offer quality services or products at reasonable prices and have good reviews from other customers.

• Follow the instructions and avoid errors. You can avoid paying unnecessary or extra fees for correcting errors, resubmitting documents, extending deadlines, appealing decisions, etc., by following the instructions and avoiding errors on your immigration application. You can also seek professional help from an immigration consultant who can help you with preparing your documents, completing your forms, submitting your application, and following up with the authorities.

In summary, paying your fees is the final step in preparing your immigration application. You need to pay the types of fees that match your program or stream and situation. You also need to pay them according to IRCC methods and instructions and avoid unnecessary or extra fees.

In Chapter 4, we will explain how to submit and track your immigration application, including submitting your application online or by mail, tracking your application status and progress, and responding to requests or issues from IRCC.

Chapter 4: Submitting and Tracking Your Immigration Application

———

IN CHAPTER 3, WE EXPLAINED how to prepare your immigration application, including gathering your documents, completing your forms, and paying your fees. In this Chapter, we will explain how to submit and track your immigration application, including submitting your application online or by mail, tracking your application status and progress, and responding to requests or issues from IRCC.

Section 1: Submitting Your Application

The first step in submitting and tracking your immigration application is to submit your application to IRCC. Your application is the official request that you make to the Canadian government for immigration to Canada. In this section, we will explain how to submit your application online or by mail, what are the advantages and disadvantages of each method, and what are the common mistakes or problems that you should avoid.

How to submit your application online?

If you apply through Express Entry or another online portal, you need to submit your application online using the IRCC website. To submit your application online, you need to:

• Create an online account on the IRCC website using your email address and a password.

• Log in to your account and access the online application portal for your program or stream.

• Fill out the digital forms online and upload the scanned copies of your documents as PDF files.

• Pay the required fees online using a valid credit card or debit card.

• Review and validate your application and make sure that everything is complete and accurate.

• Submit your application electronically and receive a confirmation message and number.

How to submit your application by mail?

If you apply outside Express Entry or another online portal, you need to submit your application by mail using a visa application centre (VAC) or another office. To submit your application by mail, you need to:

• Download and print the paper-based forms from the IRCC website or obtain them from a VAC or another office.

• Fill out the forms using a computer or a typewriter and sign them where indicated.

• Gather two copies of each document and attach them to the forms.

• Pay the required fees online using a valid credit card or debit card and print or save a copy of the receipt.

• Put everything in an envelope and label it clearly with your name, address, program or stream, and confirmation number.

- Mail your application to the address provided by IRCC or drop it off at a VAC or another office.

What are the advantages and disadvantages of each method?

The advantages and disadvantages of submitting your application online or by mail are:

- Online submission: This method is faster, easier, cheaper, safer, and more convenient. You can submit your application anytime and anywhere, save your progress and resume later, track your status and progress online, receive updates and requests by email, etc. However, this method also requires access to a computer, internet, scanner, printer, credit card or debit card, etc. You also need to follow the technical specifications and instructions carefully to avoid errors or issues.

- Mail submission: This method is slower, harder, more expensive, less safe, and less convenient. You have to wait for the mail delivery, print and sign the forms, make copies of the documents, pay for postage or courier services, etc. However, this method also does not require access to a computer, internet, scanner, printer, credit card or debit card, etc. You also do not have to worry about technical specifications or instructions as much as online submission.

What are the common mistakes or problems that you should avoid?

Some of the common mistakes or problems that you should avoid when submitting your application are:

- Submitting an incomplete or incorrect application: You should make sure that you fill out all the required forms and provide all the required documents according to IRCC instructions. You should also make sure that you provide accurate and truthful information on your forms and documents. If you submit an incomplete or incorrect application, it may be returned, refused, delayed, or cancelled.

• Submitting an outdated or expired application: You should make sure that you use the most recent version of the forms and documents available on the IRCC website. You should also make sure that you submit your application before the deadline or expiry date specified by IRCC. If you submit an outdated or expired application, it may be returned, refused, delayed, or cancelled.

• Submitting multiple applications: You should only submit one application for one program or stream at a time. You should not submit multiple applications for different programs or streams at the same time. If you do so, it may cause confusion, duplication, conflict, or cancellation of your applications.

• Submitting an unauthorized or fraudulent application: You should only submit an authorized application that is prepared by yourself or by a certified immigration consultant who has your consent and representation. You should not submit an unauthorized application that is prepared by someone else who does not have your consent or representation. You should also not submit a fraudulent application that is based on false or misleading information or documents. If you do so, it may result in serious consequences, such as refusal, revocation, removal, or criminal charges.

In summary, submitting your application is the first step in submitting and tracking your immigration application. You can submit your application online or by mail depending on your program or stream and preference. You can also avoid common mistakes or problems by submitting a complete, correct, current, and authorized application.

In Section 2, we will explain the next step in submitting and tracking your immigration application: tracking your application status and progress. We will explain how to check your application status and progress online or by phone, email, or mail, what are the different stages and timelines of the application process, and what are the factors that may affect the processing time of your application.

Section 2: Tracking Your Application Status and Progress

The next step in submitting and tracking your immigration application is to track your application status and progress. Your application status and progress are the indicators that show how your application is being processed and what stage it is at. In this section, we will explain how to check your application status and progress online or by phone, email, or mail, what are the different stages and timelines of the application process, and what are the factors that may affect the processing time of your application.

How to check your application status and progress?

You can check your application status and progress using one of the following methods:

• Online: This is the fastest and easiest way to check your application status and progress. You can use the online tools provided by IRCC on their website to access your account, view your profile, track your application, update your information, upload documents, pay fees, etc. You can also receive updates and requests by email from IRCC through this method.

• Phone: This is another way to check your application status and progress. You can call the IRCC Call Centre at 1-888-242-2100 (toll-free in Canada) or +1-613-944-4000 (outside Canada) to speak to an agent who can answer your questions and provide information about your application. You can also use the automated phone service at 1-888-242-2100 (toll-free in Canada) or +1-613-944-4000 (outside Canada) to check the status of your application using an interactive voice response system.

• Email: This is another way to check your application status and progress. You can send an email to IRCC using their web form to ask about your application. You need to provide your name, date of birth, country of birth, application number, and other details in your email. You will receive a reply from IRCC within 10 business days.

• Mail: This is another way to check your application status and progress. You can write a letter to IRCC using their mailing address to request information about your application. You need to include a copy of your passport or travel document, a copy of your receipt, a self-addressed stamped envelope, and other details in your letter. You will receive a response from IRCC within 30 business days.

What are the different stages and timelines of the application process?

The different stages and timelines of the application process depend on the program or stream that you apply under, the country or territory that you are applying from, and your personal situation. However, some common stages and timelines that apply to most immigration applications are:

• Stage 1: Submission. This is the stage when you submit your application to IRCC online or by mail. The timeline for this stage depends on how long it takes for you to prepare your application and for IRCC to receive it.

• Stage 2: Acknowledgement. This is the stage when IRCC acknowledges that they have received your application and assigns you an application number. The timeline for this stage is usually within a few days or weeks after you submit your application.

• Stage 3: Review. This is the stage when IRCC reviews your application and verifies your information and documents. The timeline for this stage varies depending on the complexity and completeness of your application and the volume of applications received by IRCC.

• Stage 4: Decision. This is the stage when IRCC makes a decision on your application based on their assessment of your eligibility and suitability for immigration to Canada. The timeline for this stage varies depending on the program or stream that you apply under and the outcome of your application.

• Stage 5: Notification. This is the stage when IRCC notifies you of their decision on your application by email or mail. The timeline for this stage is usually within a few days or weeks after they make a decision on your application.

• Stage 6: Finalization. This is the stage when IRCC finalizes your application and issues you a confirmation of permanent residence (COPR) and a visa (if applicable) that allow you to travel to Canada and land as a permanent resident. The timeline for this stage is usually within a few days or weeks after they notify you of their decision on your application.

What are the factors that may affect the processing time of your application?

The processing time of your application is the estimated time that it takes for IRCC to process your application from start to finish. The processing time may vary depending on various factors, such as:

• The program or stream that you apply under: Some programs or streams may have faster or slower processing times than others depending on their criteria, quotas, priorities, etc.

• The country or territory that you are applying from: Some countries or territories may have faster or slower processing times than others depending on their visa office capacity, security situation, service standards, etc.

• Your personal situation: Your personal situation may affect the processing time of your application depending on your background, eligibility, suitability, etc. For example, if you have a criminal record, a medical condition, a family member who is inadmissible, etc., your application may take longer to process than usual.

• Your application quality: Your application quality may affect the processing time of your application depending on how complete, accurate, consistent, and clear your application is. For example, if you provide all the required forms and documents, avoid errors or inconsistencies, respond to requests or issues promptly, etc., your application may be processed faster than usual.

You can check the current processing times for different programs or streams and countries or territories on the IRCC website. You can also use the online tools provided by IRCC on their website to track the status and progress of your specific application.

In summary, tracking your application status and progress is the next step in submitting and tracking your immigration application. You can check your application status and progress online or by phone, email, or mail using the methods and instructions provided by IRCC. You can also understand the different stages and timelines of the application process and the factors that may affect the processing time of your application.

In Section 3, we will explain the final step in submitting and tracking your immigration application: responding to requests or issues from IRCC. We will explain what types of requests or issues you may receive from IRCC, how to respond to them, and how to avoid or resolve them.

Section 3: Responding to Requests or Issues from IRCC

The final step in submitting and tracking your immigration application is to respond to requests or issues from IRCC. Requests or issues are the communications that you receive from IRCC regarding your application. They may include requests for additional information or documents, updates on your application status or progress, notifications of decisions or actions, or inquiries or concerns about your application. In this section, we will explain what types of requests or issues you may receive from IRCC, how to respond to them, and how to avoid or resolve them.

What types of requests or issues may you receive from IRCC?

The types of requests or issues that you may receive from IRCC depend on the program or stream that you apply under, the country or territory that you are applying from, and your personal situation. However, some common types of requests or issues that apply to most immigration applications are:

• Request for biometrics: This is a request that you provide your biometric data (fingerprints and photo) as part of your application. You need to provide your biometric data within 30 days of receiving this request at a designated service point in your country or territory.

• Request for medical exam: This is a request that you undergo a medical exam by a panel physician approved by the Canadian government as part of your application. You need to undergo a medical exam within 30 days of receiving this request and submit the medical exam results to IRCC.

• Request for police certificate: This is a request that you obtain a police certificate from any country or territory that you have lived in for six months or more since you turned 18 years old as part of your application. You need to obtain a police certificate within 30 days of receiving this request and submit it to IRCC.

• Request for additional information or documents: This is a request that you provide additional information or documents that are relevant to your application. For example, you may be asked to provide proof of funds, proof of relationship, proof of language proficiency, etc. You need to provide the requested information or documents within 30 days of receiving this request and submit them to IRCC.

• Update on application status or progress: This is an update that informs you of the current status or progress of your application. For example, you may be informed that your application has been received, reviewed, approved, refused, etc. You do not need to respond to this update unless instructed otherwise by IRCC.

• Notification of decision or action: This is a notification that informs you of the final decision or action taken on your application. For example, you may be notified that you have been approved for permanent residence, issued a confirmation of permanent residence (COPR) and visa (if applicable), invited to an interview or landing appointment, etc. You need to follow the instructions provided by IRCC on how to proceed with the next steps.

• Inquiry or concern about your application: This is an inquiry or concern that IRCC has about your application. For example, they may ask you to explain a discrepancy, clarify a doubt, confirm a detail, etc. You need to respond to this inquiry or concern within 30 days of receiving it and provide an honest and satisfactory explanation.

You can receive these requests or issues from IRCC by email or mail depending on how you submitted your application.

How to respond to requests or issues from IRCC?

You need to respond to requests or issues from IRCC according to the methods and instructions provided by them. You also need to make sure that your responses are timely and appropriate.

If you receive requests or issues from IRCC by email, you need to:

• Check your email regularly and look for messages from IRCC.

• Read the messages carefully and understand what they are asking for.

• Reply to the messages using the same email address that you used for your application.

• Provide the requested information or documents as attachments in PDF format.

• Use clear and concise language and avoid slang or jargon.

• Include your name, date of birth, country of birth, application number, and other details in your email.

• Keep a copy of your email and any attachments as proof of response.

If you receive requests or issues from IRCC by mail, you need to:

• Check your mail regularly and look for letters from IRCC.

• Read the letters carefully and understand what they are asking for.

• Write a letter back using the address provided by IRCC.

• Provide the requested information or documents as copies in paper format.

• Use clear and legible handwriting and avoid errors or corrections.

• Include your name, date of birth, country of birth, application number, and other details in your letter.

• Mail your letter and any copies using registered mail or courier service as proof of response.

How to avoid or resolve requests or issues from IRCC?

You can avoid or resolve requests or issues from IRCC by following these tips and best practices:

• Submit a complete and correct application: You can avoid receiving requests for additional information or documents by submitting a complete and correct application that meets the requirements and instructions of IRCC. You can also seek professional help from an immigration consultant who can help you with preparing your documents, completing your forms, submitting your application, and following up with the authorities.

• Update your information and documents: You can avoid receiving requests for updated information or documents by updating your information and documents whenever there is a change in your situation. For example, if you change your address, phone number, email address, marital status, occupation, etc., you should update your information and documents accordingly.

• Respond to requests or issues promptly and appropriately: You can resolve requests or issues from IRCC by responding to them promptly and appropriately within the given time frame and using the given method. You should also provide accurate and truthful information or documents that are relevant and satisfactory to IRCC.

• Follow the instructions and guidelines of IRCC: You can avoid or resolve requests or issues from IRCC by following the instructions and guidelines of IRCC on how to submit and track your immigration application. You should also check the IRCC website or contact the IRCC Call Centre for any questions or concerns that you may have about your application.

In summary, responding to requests or issues from IRCC is the final step in submitting and tracking your immigration application. You may receive requests or issues from IRCC by email or mail regarding your application. You need to respond to them according to IRCC methods and instructions and avoid or resolve them by submitting a complete and correct application, updating your information and documents, responding promptly and appropriately, and following the instructions and guidelines of IRCC.

In Chapter 5, we will explain how to complete and finalize your immigration process, including traveling to Canada, landing as a permanent resident, settling in Canada, and applying for Canadian citizenship.

Chapter 5: Completing and Finalizing Your Immigration Process

IN CHAPTER 4, WE EXPLAINED how to submit and track your immigration application, including submitting your application online or by mail, tracking your application status and progress, and responding to requests or issues from IRCC. In this Chapter, we will explain how to complete and finalize your immigration process, including traveling to Canada, landing as a permanent resident, settling in Canada, and applying for Canadian citizenship.

Section 1: Traveling to Canada

The first step in completing and finalizing your immigration process is to travel to Canada. Traveling to Canada is the act of entering Canada as a permanent resident or a temporary resident with the intention of becoming a permanent resident. In this section, we will explain what you need to do before, during, and after traveling to Canada, what are the documents and items that you need to bring with you, and what are the common mistakes or problems that you should avoid.

What do you need to do before traveling to Canada?

Before traveling to Canada, you need to do the following:

• Confirm your travel arrangements: You need to confirm your travel arrangements, such as your flight tickets, hotel reservations, transportation options, etc. You also need to check the travel restrictions and requirements related to COVID-19 on the IRCC website and the Government of Canada website. You may need to take a COVID-19 test, provide proof of vaccination, quarantine for 14 days, etc., depending on your situation.

• Prepare your documents and items: You need to prepare your documents and items that you need to bring with you to Canada. You also need to make copies of your important documents and leave them with someone you trust in case of loss or theft.

• Notify IRCC of any changes: You need to notify IRCC of any changes in your situation that may affect your eligibility or suitability for immigration to Canada. For example, if you change your address, phone number, email address, marital status, occupation, etc., you should update IRCC accordingly.

• Say goodbye to your family and friends: You need to say goodbye to your family and friends who are staying behind in your country or territory of origin. You may also want to celebrate your departure and thank them for their support.

What do you need to do during your trip to Canada?

During traveling to Canada, you need to do the following:

• Carry your documents and items with you: You need to carry your documents and items with you at all times. Do not put them in your checked baggage or leave them unattended. You may need to show them at various checkpoints along the way.

• Follow the rules and regulations: You need to follow the rules and regulations of the airlines, airports, border authorities, etc., that you encounter during your travel. You also need to comply with the COVID-19 measures that are in place in Canada and other countries or territories that you transit through.

• Be respectful and courteous: You need to be respectful and courteous to the staff and officials who assist you during your travel. You also need to be patient and cooperative if you face any delays or difficulties.

What do you need to do after traveling to Canada?

After traveling to Canada, you need to do the following:

• Complete your landing process: You need to complete your landing process at the port of entry (POE) in Canada. This is where you officially become a permanent resident of Canada. You need to show your confirmation of permanent residence (COPR) and visa (if applicable) and answer some questions from the border officer. You also need to declare any goods or money that you are bringing with you. You will receive a permanent resident card (PR card) by mail within a few weeks after landing.

• Settle in your destination: You need to settle in your destination in Canada. This is where you start your new life in Canada. You need to find a place to live, open a bank account, apply for a social insurance number (SIN), register for health care, enroll in school or work, etc. You can also access various settlement services and programs that can help you with your integration.

What are the documents and items that you need to bring with you?

The documents and items that you need to bring with you depend on your program or stream, your country or territory of origin, and your personal situation. However, some common documents and items that apply to most immigration applications are:

• Documents:

o Passport or travel document

o Confirmation of permanent residence (COPR) and visa (if applicable)

o Proof of funds

o Proof of vaccination (if applicable)

o Medical exam results (if applicable)

o Police certificates (if applicable)

o Education documents

o Work documents

o Language test results

o Other documents

- Items:

o Clothes

o Toiletries

o Medications

o Electronics

o Money

o Jewelry

o Photos

o Other items

You can find the list of specific documents and items that you need to bring with you on the IRCC website or in the document checklist that is included in the application package.

What are the common mistakes or problems that you should avoid?

Some of the common mistakes or problems that you should avoid when traveling to Canada are:

• Traveling without valid documents or items: You should make sure that you have valid documents or items that are required for your travel and entry to Canada. You should also make sure that they are not damaged, expired, or missing. If you travel without valid documents or items, you may be denied boarding, entry, or landing in Canada.

• Traveling with prohibited or restricted goods or money: You should make sure that you do not bring any goods or money that are prohibited or restricted by the Canadian laws and regulations. For example, you should not bring any weapons, drugs, plants, animals, etc., that are illegal or harmful in Canada. You should also declare any goods or money that exceed the limit set by the Canadian customs. If you travel with prohibited or restricted goods or money, you may face penalties, confiscation, or criminal charges.

• Traveling with false or misleading information or documents: You should make sure that you do not provide any false or misleading information or documents to the airlines, airports, border authorities, etc., that you encounter during your travel. For example, you should not lie, omit, or falsify any information or documents about your identity, eligibility, suitability, etc., for immigration to Canada. If you travel with false or misleading information or documents, you may face serious consequences, such as refusal, revocation, removal, or criminal charges.

In summary, traveling to Canada is the first step in completing and finalizing your immigration process. You need to do some things before, during, and after traveling to Canada to ensure a smooth and successful journey. You also need to bring the documents and items that are required for your travel and entry to Canada and avoid the mistakes or problems that may cause trouble or delay.

In Section 2, we will explain the next step in completing and finalizing your immigration process: landing as a permanent resident. We will explain what landing as a permanent resident means, what are the rights and responsibilities of a permanent resident, and what are the steps and tips for landing as a permanent resident.

Section 2: Landing as a Permanent Resident

The next step in completing and finalizing your immigration process is to land as a permanent resident. Landing as a permanent resident is the act of confirming your status as a permanent resident of Canada at the port of entry (POE) or at an inland office. In this section, we will explain what landing as a permanent resident means, what are the rights and responsibilities of a permanent resident, and what are the steps and tips for landing as a permanent resident.

What does landing as a permanent resident mean?

Landing as a permanent resident means that you officially become a permanent resident of Canada. A permanent resident is someone who has been granted the right to live, work, and study in Canada indefinitely, but is not a Canadian citizen. A permanent resident has most of the same rights and responsibilities as a Canadian citizen, except for some differences, such as voting, running for office, holding certain jobs, etc.

Landing as a permanent resident is different from traveling to Canada or entering Canada. Traveling to Canada or entering Canada is the act of arriving in Canada as a temporary resident or a permanent resident. A temporary resident is someone who has been granted the right to visit, work, or study in Canada for a limited period of time, such as a visitor, worker, or student. A temporary resident has fewer rights and responsibilities than a permanent resident or a Canadian citizen.

Landing as a permanent resident is also different from becoming a Canadian citizen. Becoming a Canadian citizen is the act of acquiring Canadian citizenship by birth or by naturalization. A Canadian citizen is someone who has full rights and responsibilities as a member of the

Canadian society, such as voting, running for office, holding any job, etc. A Canadian citizen also has the right to hold a Canadian passport and receive consular protection abroad.

What are the rights and responsibilities of a permanent resident?

The rights and responsibilities of a permanent resident are:

- Rights:

    o Live, work, and study anywhere in Canada

    o Access health care and social services

    o Apply for Canadian citizenship after meeting the eligibility criteria

    o Be protected by Canadian laws and the Canadian Charter of Rights and Freedoms

- Responsibilities:

    o Pay taxes and respect Canadian laws.

    o Learn English or French and integrate into Canadian society.

    o Maintain your permanent resident status by meeting the residency obligation.

    o Carry your permanent resident card (PR card) when traveling outside Canada.

What are the steps and tips for landing as a permanent resident?

The steps and tips for landing as a permanent resident are:

• Step 1: Prepare for landing. You need to prepare for landing by doing the following:

> o Check your confirmation of permanent residence (COPR) and visa (if applicable) and make sure that they are valid and not expired.

> o Book your flight or transportation to Canada and make sure that you arrive before the expiry date of your COPR or visa.

> o Pack your documents and items that you need to bring with you to Canada, such as your passport, COPR, visa, proof of funds, etc.

> o Plan your destination and accommodation in Canada and make sure that you have enough money to cover your initial expenses.

• Step 2: Arrive at the port of entry (POE) in Canada. You need to arrive at the POE in Canada by doing the following:

> o Present your passport, COPR, visa (if applicable), and other documents or items to the border officer.

> o Answer some questions from the border officer about your identity, eligibility, suitability, etc., for immigration to Canada.

o Declare any goods or money that you are bringing with you to Canada using the declaration card or kiosk.

o Receive your COPR with an entry stamp and date that confirms your landing as a permanent resident.

• Step 3: Settle in Canada. You need to settle in Canada by doing the following:

o Find a place to live temporarily or permanently in Canada.

o Apply for a social insurance number (SIN) at a Service Canada office or online.

o Register for health care coverage at a provincial or territorial health ministry office or online.

o Enroll in school or work in Canada according to your qualifications and credentials.

o Access settlement services and programs that can help you with your integration in Canada.

Some tips and best practices for landing as a permanent resident are:

• Be prepared and organized: You should be prepared and organized for landing as a permanent resident by having all your documents and items ready and accessible. You should also have copies of your important documents in case of loss or theft.

• Be honest and cooperative: You should be honest and cooperative with the border officer who handles your landing process. You should provide accurate and truthful information and documents that match your application. You should also follow their instructions and requests.

• Be patient and flexible: You should be patient and flexible with the landing process as it may take some time depending on various factors, such as the volume of travelers, the security situation, the COVID-19 measures, etc. You should also be ready to adapt to any changes or challenges that may arise.

In summary, landing as a permanent resident is the next step in completing and finalizing your immigration process. You need to do some things before, during, and after landing as a permanent resident to ensure a smooth and successful transition. You also need to understand the rights and responsibilities of a permanent resident and follow the steps and tips for landing as a permanent resident.

In Section 3, we will explain the final step in completing and finalizing your immigration process: settling in Canada. We will explain what settling in Canada means, what are the challenges and opportunities of settling in Canada, and what are the resources and tips for settling in Canada.

Section 3: Settling in Canada

The final step in completing and finalizing your immigration process is to settle in Canada. Settling in Canada is the act of adapting and integrating into the Canadian society and culture as a permanent resident. In this section, we will explain what settling in Canada means, what are the challenges and opportunities of settling in Canada, and what are the resources and tips for settling in Canada.

What does settling in Canada mean?

Settling in Canada means that you start your new life in Canada as a permanent resident. It involves finding a place to live, opening a bank account, registering for health care, enrolling in school or work, learning English or French, making friends, joining community activities, etc. It also involves learning about the Canadian values, laws, rights, responsibilities, history, geography, etc., and respecting the diversity and multiculturalism of the Canadian society.

Settling in Canada is different from landing as a permanent resident or becoming a Canadian citizen. Landing as a permanent resident is the act of confirming your status as a permanent resident of Canada at the port of entry (POE) or at an inland office. Becoming a Canadian citizen is the act of acquiring Canadian citizenship by birth or by naturalization.

Settling in Canada is also different from visiting, working, or studying in Canada. Visiting, working, or studying in Canada is the act of staying in Canada for a limited period of time as a temporary resident, such as a visitor, worker, or student. A temporary resident has fewer rights and responsibilities than a permanent resident or a Canadian citizen.

THE ULTIMATE GUIDE TO CANADIAN IMMIGRATION PATHWAYS

What are the challenges and opportunities of settling in Canada?

The challenges and opportunities of settling in Canada depend on your program or stream, your country or territory of origin, and your personal situation. However, some common challenges and opportunities that apply to most immigration applications are:

- Challenges:

  o Language barrier: You may face difficulties in communicating with others or accessing services or information if you do not speak English or French fluently. You may also face discrimination or isolation if you do not understand the cultural norms or expectations of the Canadian society.

  o Culture shock: You may experience stress, anxiety, confusion, frustration, or depression as you adjust to the new environment and lifestyle in Canada. You may also feel homesick, lonely, or nostalgic for your country or territory of origin.

  o Employment gap: You may have trouble finding a job or advancing your career in Canada if you do not have Canadian work experience, qualifications, credentials, references, etc. You may also face competition or discrimination from other job seekers or employers.

  o Financial hardship: You may struggle to pay for your living expenses, such as rent, food, transportation, utilities, etc., especially if you do not have a stable income or savings. You may also have to deal with taxes, debts, loans, etc., that may affect your financial situation.

o Family separation: You may miss your family members who are not with you in Canada or who are still waiting for their immigration applications to be processed. You may also have difficulties in maintaining contact or supporting them from afar.

- Opportunities:

o Language learning: You can improve your English or French skills by taking language classes, joining language clubs, watching TV shows or movies, reading books or newspapers, listening to podcasts or music, etc. You can also learn other languages spoken by different communities in Canada.

o Cultural diversity: You can learn about and appreciate the cultural diversity and multiculturalism of the Canadian society by meeting people from different backgrounds, religions, ethnicities, etc., attending cultural events or festivals, visiting museums or landmarks, trying new foods or cuisines, etc. You can also share your own culture and heritage with others.

o Employment potential: You can find a job or advance your career in Canada by using your skills, education, work experience, etc., that you have acquired from your country or territory of origin. You can also upgrade your qualifications, credentials, references, etc., by taking courses or programs offered by various institutions in Canada.

o Financial security: You can achieve financial security and stability in Canada by managing your budget wisely and saving for your future goals. You can also access various financial services and benefits offered by the Canadian government and other organizations in Canada.

o Family reunification: You can reunite with your family members who are not with you in Canada or who are still waiting for their immigration applications to be processed by sponsoring them under the family class immigration program. You can also maintain contact and support them by using various communication tools and methods.

What are the resources and tips for settling in Canada?

The resources and tips for settling in Canada are:

• Resources:

o Settlement services and programs: These are services and programs that can help you with your settlement and integration in Canada. They include language classes, employment assistance, orientation sessions, counseling services, mentoring programs, etc. They are offered by various government agencies and non-governmental organizations (NGOs) across Canada. You can find and access them online or in person.

o Settlement workers: These are workers who can help you with your settlement and integration in Canada. They include settlement counselors, language instructors, employment consultants, etc. They work for various settlement services and programs across Canada. You can contact and consult them online or in person.

o Settlement guides and tools: These are guides and tools that can help you with your settlement and integration in Canada. They include websites, apps, videos, podcasts, books, etc. They provide information and advice on various topics related to settlement and integration in Canada. You can access and use them online or offline.

• Tips:

o Be prepared and proactive: You should be prepared and proactive for settling in Canada by doing some research and planning before and after your arrival. You should also seek and use the resources and tips that are available for settling in Canada.

o Be open and curious: You should be open and curious about settling in Canada by exploring and experiencing the new environment and lifestyle in Canada. You should also learn and appreciate the cultural diversity and multiculturalism of Canadian society.

o Be positive and resilient: You should be positive and resilient about settling in Canada by overcoming the challenges and seizing the opportunities that come with settling in Canada. You should also celebrate your achievements and milestones as you settle in Canada.

In summary, settling in Canada is the final step in completing and finalizing your immigration process. You need to do some things before, during, and after settling in Canada to ensure a smooth and successful transition. You also need to understand the challenges and opportunities of settling in Canada and use the resources and tips for settling in Canada.

In Section 4, we will explain how to apply for Canadian citizenship after meeting the eligibility criteria. We will explain what Canadian citizenship means, what are the benefits and responsibilities of a Canadian citizen, and what are the steps and tips for applying for Canadian citizenship.

Section 4: Applying for Canadian Citizenship

The final step in completing and finalizing your immigration process is to apply for Canadian citizenship. Applying for Canadian citizenship is the act of requesting to become a Canadian citizen by naturalization. In this section, we will explain what Canadian citizenship means, what are the benefits and responsibilities of a Canadian citizen, and what are the steps and tips for applying for Canadian citizenship.

What does Canadian citizenship mean?

Canadian citizenship means that you are a full member of the Canadian society and have the same rights and responsibilities as those who are born in Canada. A Canadian citizen is someone who has acquired Canadian citizenship by birth or by naturalization. A Canadian citizen has the right to hold a Canadian passport and receive consular protection abroad. A Canadian citizen also has the right to vote, run for office, hold any job, etc.

Canadian citizenship is different from permanent residency or temporary residency. Permanent residency is the status of someone who has been granted the right to live, work, and study in Canada indefinitely, but is not a Canadian citizen. A permanent resident has most of the same rights and responsibilities as a Canadian citizen, except for some differences, such as voting, running for office, holding certain jobs, etc. Temporary residency is the status of someone who has been granted the right to visit, work, or study in Canada for a limited period of time, such as a visitor, worker, or student. A temporary resident has fewer rights and responsibilities than a permanent resident or a Canadian citizen.

What are the benefits and responsibilities of a Canadian citizen?

The benefits and responsibilities of a Canadian citizen are:

• Benefits:

o Travel freely: You can travel freely to and from Canada without any restrictions or limitations. You can also travel to many countries or territories around the world without a visa or with a visa on arrival using your Canadian passport.

o Vote and run for office: You can vote and run for office at the federal, provincial, territorial, and municipal levels of government in Canada. You can also participate in other democratic activities, such as petitions, referendums, consultations, etc.

o Hold any job: You can hold any job in Canada that requires or prefers Canadian citizenship, such as working for the federal government, the military, the police, etc.

o Receive consular protection: You can receive consular protection from the Canadian government when you are traveling or living abroad. You can also access various services and benefits offered by the Canadian government and other organizations abroad.

o Pass on your citizenship: You can pass on your citizenship to your children who are born outside Canada under certain conditions.

• Responsibilities:

o Obey the law: You must obey the law and respect the rights and freedoms of others in Canada. You must also follow the laws and regulations of other countries or territories that you visit or live in.

o Pay taxes: You must pay taxes to support the public services and programs that benefit you and others in Canada. You must also report your income and assets to the Canadian government and pay taxes on them if applicable.

o Serve on a jury: You may be called to serve on a jury in a criminal or civil trial in Canada. You must perform your duty as a juror honestly and impartially.

o Protect the environment: You should protect the environment and conserve natural resources in Canada and elsewhere. You should also reduce your environmental impact and support environmental initiatives.

o Contribute to society: You should contribute to society and make Canada a better place for yourself and others. You should also celebrate your diversity and multiculturalism and promote peace and harmony.

What are the steps and tips for applying for Canadian citizenship?

The steps and tips for applying for Canadian citizenship are:

• Step 1: Check your eligibility. You need to check your eligibility by meeting the following criteria:

o Be at least 18 years old.

o Be a permanent resident of Canada.

o Have lived in Canada for at least three out of the last five years.

o Have filed your taxes for at least three out of the last five years.

o Have adequate knowledge of English or French

o Have adequate knowledge of Canada's history, geography, government, etc.

o Have no criminal record or security issues.

• Step 2: Prepare your application. You need to prepare your application by doing the following:

o Download and fill out the application forms from the IRCC website or obtain them from an IRCC office.

o Gather two copies of each document that supports your application, such as your passport, PR card, tax returns, language test results, etc.

o Pay the required fees online using a valid credit card or debit card and print or save a copy of the receipt.

o Put everything in an envelope and label it clearly with your name, address, program or stream, and confirmation number.

• Step 3: Submit your application. You need to submit your application by doing the following:

o Mail your application to the address provided by IRCC or drop it off at an IRCC office.

o Receive an acknowledgement letter from IRCC that confirms the receipt of your application and assigns you an application number.

o Wait for IRCC to process your application and notify you of the next steps.

• Step 4: Take the citizenship test and interview. You need to take the citizenship test and interview by doing the following:

o Receive an invitation letter from IRCC that informs you of the date, time, and location of your citizenship test and interview.

o Study for the citizenship test using the official study guide and other resources provided by IRCC.

o Attend the citizenship test and answer 20 multiple-choice questions about Canada's history, geography, government, etc., in 30 minutes.

o Attend the citizenship interview and answer some questions from the citizenship officer about your identity, eligibility, suitability, etc., for Canadian citizenship.

o Receive a decision letter from IRCC that informs you of the result of your citizenship test and interview.

• Step 5: Attend the citizenship ceremony. You need to attend the citizenship ceremony by doing the following:

o Receive a notice letter from IRCC that invites you to attend a citizenship ceremony in your area.

o Bring your original documents and items that you need to bring with you to the citizenship ceremony, such as your passport, PR card, invitation letter, etc.

o Take the oath of citizenship and receive your certificate of citizenship that confirms your Canadian citizenship.

o Celebrate your Canadian citizenship and enjoy your new rights and responsibilities.

Some tips and best practices for applying for Canadian citizenship are:

• Be prepared and organized: You should be prepared and organized for applying for Canadian citizenship by having all your documents and items ready and accessible. You should also have copies of your important documents in case of loss or theft.

• Be honest and cooperative: You should be honest and cooperative with IRCC who handles your citizenship application. You should provide accurate and truthful information and documents that match your application. You should also follow their instructions and requests.

• Be patient and flexible: You should be patient and flexible with the citizenship application process as it may take some time depending on various factors, such as the volume of applications, the security situation, the COVID-19 measures, etc. You should also be ready to adapt to any changes or challenges that may arise.

In summary, applying for Canadian citizenship is the final step in completing and finalizing your immigration process. You need to do some things before, during, and after applying for Canadian citizenship to ensure a smooth and successful transition. You also need to understand the benefits and responsibilities of a Canadian citizen and follow the steps and tips for applying for Canadian citizenship.

Conclusion

THIS CONCLUDES CHAPTER 5 and this book on how to immigrate to Canada.

We hope that you have enjoyed it and found it useful for your immigration process. We also hope that you have gained more confidence and motivation to pursue your immigration goals and start your new life in Canada.

This book is not intended to provide legal advice or representation for your immigration application. Should you require an immigration consultant or lawyer for professional help with your immigration application, quickly go to https://www.ImmigrateWithPeace.com and book a consultation session.

This book is also not intended to be exhaustive or comprehensive of all the information and resources related to immigration to Canada. You should always check the IRCC website or contact the IRCC Call Centre for the most updated and accurate information and resources related to your immigration application. You can also book a consultation session with me here[1].

Thank you for reading through this book. We wish you all the best in your immigration journey and your new life in Canada. I look forward to hearing from you soon.

---

1. https://www.ImmigrateWithPeace.com

About the Author

I am Mrs. Gloria Morenike Faluyi-Ogieva, an Internationally trained Lawyer in Alberta, Canada. A graduate of University of Abuja, Nigeria and the Osgood Law School, York University, Canada, I started my career as a lawyer in 2011 back in Nigeria and relocated to Canada with my family in 2018.

As a Barrister & Solicitor in Canada with over 12 years of legal experience, I've dedicated my career to making a positive impact through law. My expertise spans across various legal realms, but my passion lies in Family Law, Immigration Law, and Real Estate.

Throughout my journey, I've had the privilege of representing clients from diverse corners of the world, helping them find tailored solutions to their unique legal needs.

But that's not all. Considering the rigorous path that led to my immigration to Canada and admittance to the Canadian Bar, I decided to establish Immigrate with Peace - a firm committed to providing Immigration and Visa advisory services globally. I use this platform to help intending immigrants to achieve their immigration dreams with peace of mind and zero stress.

My mission is crystal clear: to champion justice, advocate for equitable immigration laws and policies, elevate the standards of immigration services, and above all, serve you, our valued clients, with excellence.

Do you have immigration needs on your horizon? Whether it's your dream of permanent residency, pursuing education in Canada, the UK, or the US, Travel Visas, Business Registration, LMIA applications, or Refugee Appeal hearings, consider me your go-to ally.

Simply visit https://immigratewithpeace.com/ to schedule a consultation session with me. Let's embark on this journey together and turn your dreams into a reality.

Thank you for reading this book. I look forward to connecting with you, addressing your immigration needs, and making your dreams come true!

Read more at https://immigratewithpeace.com.

About the Publisher

KA Publishing is a leading provider of resources, books, courses, and trainings for individuals and businesses who seek to grow and develop in the areas of internet marketing and online business, inspiration and motivation, book summaries, and education. We are committed to providing high-quality, informative content that inspires, educates, and empowers our readers to achieve their personal, professional and corporate goals.

Read more at https://kapublishing.com/.

www.ingramcontent.com/pod-product-compliance
Lightning Source LLC
Chambersburg PA
CBHW071329140726
47996CB00005B/1898